iPhone 12

User Guide

Perfect Guide for Beginners, & Seniors to Become Experts of iPhone 12 Mini, iPhone 12, iPhone 12 Pro & iPhone 12 Pro Max Running with Latest iOS 14 within 24 Hours

Ephong Globright

Copyright © 2020

Facts Acclamation

This iPhone 12 User Manual is primarily designed to provide complete solutions to several operational challenges on the use of many basic apps, technical setup, ensuring comfortability, and safe usage of the iPhone by the dummies, beginners, and seniors.

TABLE OF CONTENTS

5

INTRODUCTION

This iPhone 12 Mini, iPhone 12, iPhone 12 Pro, and iPhone 12 Pro Max User Guide contains everything that is very important for dummies, beginners, and seniors to become the masters of the newly released iPhone running iOS 14.

This Manual completely simplified all the steps with clear pictures; screenshots, easy to understand tips, and trick to solve every problem in the terms of:

> *Manual or Automatic Setup of your new iPhone to start working,*
> *Changing of Default Settings,*
> *Selection of best Timer or Clock,*
> *Customizing Controls in Control Center,*
> *Choosing of Attractive Wallpaper,*
> *Creating of 3 in 1 Feature on Homescreen including Location Forecast Weather, Calendar and News Platform;*
> *Upgrading of Old iPhone of iOS Version to Current iOS Version,*
> *Increasing or Decreasing of Homepages, Rearrangement of Application (App) Icons,*
> *Creating Apple ID, Face ID & Passcode,*
> *Transferring data from Android Phone to iPhone 12/Mini/Max,*
> *Production of Professional Photos with help of in-Built Camera.*
> *Customized Animoji,*
> *Identifying App's Icons and their Functions*
> *Using of Siri, Lost My, Carplay, FaceTime for Conference Video Call, iMessage, ProCam App, Health App... and many others.*

There are a lot more tips you will learn to ease the use of your iPhone. The iPhone is more loaded with many amazing features on iOS 14 that make life lovely and fulfilling for every iPhone 12, Pro Mini, and Pro Max user.

Due to several health complications the world is currently confronting, many iPhone users had thought that the second-generation iPhone SE 2020 would only be the iPhone that would be released this year 2020 without knowing that more of the amazing innovative iPhones that will be running with advanced iOS 14 was in progress.

Until October 13 2020 four different iPhones such as iPhone 12, 12 Mini, 12 Pro, and 12 Pro Max respectively were introduced in different sizes and surprisingly released by Apple Company to improve user comfortability and wellbeing.

The latest benefits include the Forecasting Weather icon of the different locations on the Home page to guide every individual on how to prepare for his/her daily movement, in fact, this adds multiple ovations to Apple Company.

This shows that as a user you could determine the climatic weather conditions of the place you are going. The temperature of the environment, humidity, and name of the location will be displayed on the screen for a proper guide if you enable the widget. However, details were to be discussed later in the book.

In the Manual you will have complete answers to the following questions:

1. *What is special about the latest iOS 14?*
2. *How could the latest iPhone safely charge without using a USB Charging Cord and Adapter?*
3. *What is the battery quality?*
4. *Are they quality than their immediate predecessors such as iPhone 11, 11 Pro, and 11 Pro Max respectively?*
5. *What are the advancements in Rear and Front Facing Camera?*
6. *What is the depth distance of water that the latest iPhone could endure and how long could it last in there?*
7. *What is the memory capacity?*
8. *... and so on.*

As a beginner or a senior iPhone User, be rest assure that everything you need to know about your newly purchased iPhone 12, Mini, Pro, and Max was clearly discussed below step by step without missing out on any important facts.

Let me start with the general introduction of the external parts of the four iPhones. I separated iPhones that have different physical components for proper differentiation of the four iPhones.

For instance, iPhone 12 Mini and iPhone 12 have many things in common while iPhone 12 Pro and iPhone 12 Pro Max also have more things in common in terms of look, cameras, and display.

Also, note that the four of them have the same method of operational activities because they are all using the same iOS 14 that determines their functions and general beneficial features.

About the Special Body Structures

The iPhone 12, Mini, Pro, and Max body shapes are slightly redesigned to be more portable, attractive, and durable in preventing edges from cracking when fall.

Manufactured Color

The iPhone 12 Mini and iPhone 12 come in **black, white, red, green, and blue body appearances.**

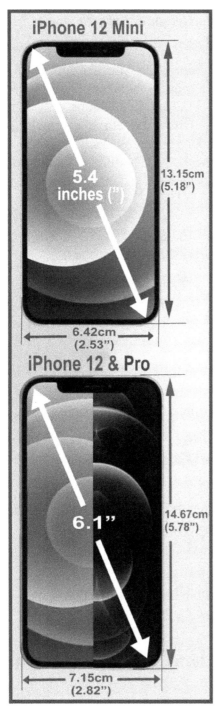

The iPhone 12 Pro and Pro Max come in **silver, graphite, gold, and pacific blue body appearances.**

IP68 Waterproof and Dustproof Certification

The four iPhones could endure a maximum depth of 6 meters of water for approximately 30 minutes.

The iPhone Weight
1. The iPhone 12 Mini 135 grams (4.76 ounces)
2. The iPhone 12 weighs 164 grams (5.78 ounces).
3. The iPhone 12 Pro weighs 189 grams (6.66 ounces).
4. The iPhone 12 Pro Max weighs 228 grams (8.03 ounces).

General Screen Display

Screen Diagonal Size: The iPhone 12 Mini comes with 5.4 inches of Super Retina Extreme Dynamic Range (XDR) Screen Diagonal.

The iPhone 12 & 12 Pro come with 6.1 inches Super Retina XDR Screen Diagonal.

The iPhone 12 Pro Max comes with 6.7 inches Super Retina XDR Screen Diagonal.

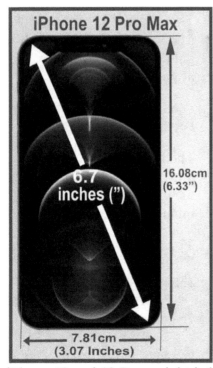

Height & Breadth

1. The iPhone 12 Mini comes with 13.15cm (5.18 Inches) x 6.42cm (2.53 Inches).

2. The iPhone 12 comes with 14.67cm (5.78 Inches) x 7.15cm (2.82 Inches).

3. The iPhone 12 Pro come with 14.67cm (5.78 Inches) x 7.15cm (2.82 Inches).

4. The iPhone 12 Pro Max 16.08cm (6.33 Inches) x 7.81cm (3.07 Inches).

The four iPhones have a Contrast Ratio of 2,000,000:1 of Organic Light Emitted Diode (OLED).

iPhone 12 and 12 Pro-weight is heavier than the iPhone 11 iPhone because the frame is made up of steel stainless while the iPhone 12 Mini and 12 are made up of the Aluminum frame.

The iPhone 12, Mini, Pro & Max have a *Ceramic Shield Glass* to endure four-time protection of the iPhones from damage when they fall unconsciously.

They all have True Tone Display, P3 Wide Color Display, and Hepatic Touch.

Brightness Strength

The iPhone 12 and Mini typically have 625nits maximum brightness while the iPhone 12 Pro and Pro Max have 800nits maximum brightness and iPhone.

They are all having the same Maximum Brightness of 1200nits High Dynamic Range (HDR).

The iPhone 12 Mini has an HDR display of 2340 by 1080 pixel resolution at 476 pixels per inch (PPI).

The iPhone 12 & Pro has an HDR display of 2532 by 1170 pixel resolution at 460ppi.

The iPhone Pro Max has an HDR display of 2778 by 1284 pixel resolution at 458ppi.

A14 Bionic Support 5G Network Technology

The A14 Bionic has a capacity of 11.8 billion transistors with the highest speed of the Central Processing Unit (CPU), Graphics Processing Unit (GPU), and 80.37% Superfast Natural Engine.

All four iPhones could be used with 5G SIM which is the current fastest communication network service technology of this period.

This enables the mega-high speed of downloading and uploading with high-quality streaming activities on your iPhone.

A14 Bionic also improves maximum efficiency of transferring data, and network connectivity (No network interruption or Failure by the iPhone except the service provider).

Memory Storage

The iPhone 12 and Mini

Both iPhones come with these various capacities of 64GB, 128GB, and 256GB. The higher the memory capacity in the iPhone, the more the price of the iPhone because the storage size of the memory determines the cost of the iPhone.

The iPhone 12 Pro and Max

Both iPhones come with these various capacities of 128GB, 256GB, and 512GB

Rear (Back) Cameras

The iPhone 12 and Mini

Cameras: The iPhone 12 and Mini rear cameras comprises dual camera of Ultra Wide and Wide Camera.

i. The 12MP Ultra Wide Camera can cover 120^0 Field View with the help of 5-Element Lens, f/2.4 Aperture, and 13mm Focal Length.

ii. The 12MP Wide Camera has absolute Focus Pixels, stabilized optical imageability with the aid of sensor-shift, 7-elements of f/1.6 Aperture, and 26mm Focal Length

Video Version: They have Dolby Vision HDR video with the ability to record approximately 30 fps

Zoom Magnification: The iPhone 12 and Max have an optical zoom range of four times (4x)

The iPhone 12 Pro and Max

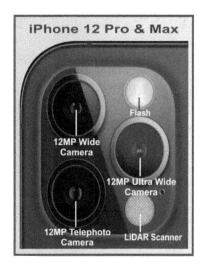

Cameras: They have three different 12MP Cameras that include Ultra Wide, Wide, and Telephoto Cameras.

i. The 12MP Camera uses a 5-element lens with a 13mm focal length to cover a 120° field of view with f/2.4 Aperture.

ii. The 12MP Wide Camera has an absolute Focus Pixel, Stabilizing Optical Image with the help of sensor-shift, 7-Elements Lens of 26mm Focal Length with

14

unto 27 percent improved low light capacity.

iii. The 12MP Telephoto Camera uses a 6-element lens with a distance capacity of 52mm focal length, stabilizing optical image, 4 times optical zoom range, and f/2.0 Aperture.

Zoom Magnification: The iPhone 12 Pro has an optical zoom range of four times (4x) while iPhone 12 Pro Max has a capacity of the optical zoom range of six times (6x)

Apple ProRAW: This is designed for an iPhone user using a professional camera to take massive raw images; provides a large file to save the collective Raw images on your iPhone. It will also enable you to edit your images and save them as JPEG documents.

It adds different color effects on the image during raw image display.

It also has a *Light Detection and Ranging (LiDAR)* Scanner for Night Mode Portrait, rapid autofocus in poor light to produce distinct background and cop-out the real images, and carry-out next stage of Augmented Reality (AR).

It could be used to rearrange the position of the images on your portrait coverage.

When press and hold any farther image, move it close to the other image(s) to remove in-between distance.

Video Recording Capacity

The iPhone 12, Mini, Pro & Max

1. They have 4K Video recording at 24 frames per second (fps), 30 fps, or 60 fps.
2. They have 1080p HD Video recording capacity that could record at 30 fps or 60 fps.
3. The high dynamic range (HDR) could record with Dolby Vision at approximately 30 fps.
4. They have an extended dynamic range that could record approximately 60 fps.

15

5. They are all having Video Optical Image & Time-lapse stabilization.
6. **Zoom Magnification:**
    - The iPhone 12 & Mini have optical zoom out of times two and times three of digital zoom up.
    - The iPhone 12 Pro has optical zoom out & in of times two and times six of digital zoom up.
    - The iPhone 12 Pro Max has optical zoom out of time two and a half, and zoon in times two with times seven digital zoom up.
7. They all have a QuickTake Video feature.
8. They all have Slo-Mo (Slow Motion) Video of 1080p at the rate of 120 fps or 240 fps.
9. They are all having Audio and Stereo recording features

Front-Facing Camera

The iPhone 12, Mini, Pro, and Max

1. The four smartphones have super-quality of 12 Megapixel (MP) image productions, TrueDepth Camera with f/2.2 Aperture.
2. The Photos have Smart HDR 3, Portrait mode with advanced Bokeh and Depth Control.
3. They have 4K, 1080p, and 720p of cinematic video stabilizing capacity.
4. 4K Video recording at the rate of 24 fps, 30 fps, or 60 fps.

However, the front-facing camera has the same functions and capabilities as rear cameras.

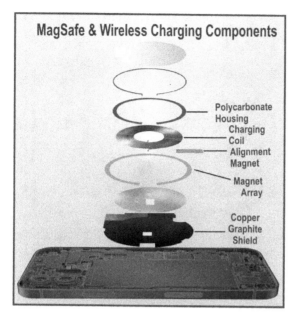

MagSafe & Wireless Charging Components

Polycarbonate Housing
Charging Coil
Alignment Magnet
Magnet Array
Copper Graphite Shield

It is one of the outstanding improvements in the current iPhone 12 Mini, 12, 12 Pro, and 12 Pro Max that have the same number of **Megapixels** of Rear and Front Facing Camera.

Therefore, you could completely perform everything you could do with the rear cameras.

The Lighting Feature Effects

They all have six distinct lighting effects to beautify your photos.

MagSafe Charger & Wireless Charger

Wireless Charger: The is a magnetic charger that quickly charges iPhone with the help of the in-built magnetic components at the back of the iPhone that sends electric charge into the iPhone charging coil which in turn transfer power to the battery.

Connection

- Get or Buy Apple 20Watt (W) USB-C Power Adapter or other acceptable power adapter and connect the MagSafe Charger which is not coming with the iPhone 12.
- Remove the Wireless Charger from its wallet.
- Put the MagSafe Charger at the center back of the iPhone. If you are using MagSafe Case position the charger inside the designed face at the back.
- Let your iPhone face up.
- In a second, a circular green will show on the iPhone screen to indicate the charging level.

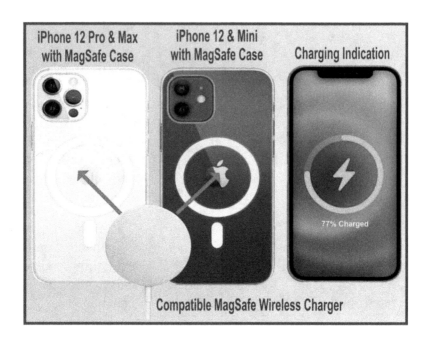

iPhone 12 Pro & Max with MagSafe Case

iPhone 12 & Mini with MagSafe Case

Charging Indication

77% Charged

Compatible MagSafe Wireless Charger

Battery Capacity

Battery Size

The iPhone 12 Mini comes with a battery size of 2227mAh

The iPhone 12 and Pro come with a battery size of 2815mAh

The iPhone 12 Pro Max comes with a battery size 3687mAh

The iPhone 12, Mini, Pro, and Max have rechargeable built-in Lithium-ion batteries with an hour different power capacity.

The iPhone 12 and Pro have two hours more power capacity than iPhone 12 Mini, while the iPhone 12 Pro Max has five hours more power capacity than iPhone 12 Mini.

Streamed Audio & Video Playback

The iPhone 12 Mini can stream playback audio sound for closely 50 hours and stream playback video for 10 hours.

The iPhone 12 and Pro have the same ability to stream playback audio for 65 hours and video for 11 hours.

The iPhone 12 Max has more ability to stream playback audio for 80 hours and video could last up to 12 hours.

Charging Duration

The four iPhones could be approximately charged up to 50% within 30minutes when you use Apple 20W USB-C Power Adapter or other compatible higher adapter recommended.

You could get the original and reliable power adapter on Amazon.com or Verizon.com.

Components of the iPhone 12, Mini, Pro, and Max Notch

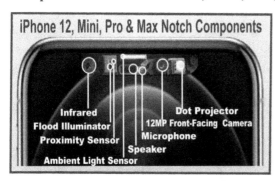

The Notch location is the top black center of your iPhone where there is a Face Sensor, Stereo Speaker with Microphone, and Front-Facing Camera.

Face Sensor: This recognizes the original owner's face that has been captured and saved for Face ID during setup or later performed in the Settings. The sensor will be displaying blinking infrared light to scan your face for the lock screen of your iPhone to be unlocked.

Stereo Speaker with In-Build Microphone: This will enable you to hear the audible sound and send voice sound to anyone calling you. It also helps during live-voice recording.

Front-Facing Camera: The camera comes with more improved megapixels of 12 and is designed to capture every image or object at the front of your iPhone screen including moving objects or living things like animals, plants, and humans. Therefore, you can use the Front-Facing Camera to take a personal picture called Selfie directly without asking for any external support.

Documents You Can Access on Your iPhone

There are documents you access on your iPhone 11, 11 Pro, or 11 Pro Max without looking for a format converter. Any of the accepted documents can be used or shared on the website page, mail, social media platform or to compose a message on your iPhone as a reminder or planner… and many others.

The documents are:

1. Microsoft Excel of XISX and XIS
2. Microsoft PowerPoint of PPTX
3. Microsoft Word of DOCX and DOC
4. Text of TXT
5. Image of JPG, GIF, TIFF;
6. USDZ Universal of USDZ, ZIP, and ICS
7. Keynote of KEY
8. Preview and Adobe Acrobat Document Format of PDF
9. Contact information of VCF
10. Rich Text Format or RTF
11. Numbers of NUMBERS format.
12. Web Pages of HTML and HTM

Compatible SIM Card

You can perfectly use *Dual SIM* that includes nano-SIM and eSIM (Embedded SIM) in any of the four iPhones. But you cannot use

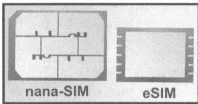

micro-SIM cards on any of the iPhones.

How to insert the dual SIM or single compatible SIM will be fully discussed in Chapter One before you move on to the next level of systematic iPhone setup steps.

The Uses of All the Buttons Surrounding iPhone 12, Mini, Pro & Max

Power Button: The power button is located at the top right side of the iPhone. It is sometimes called the Switch button or Siri button.

Power Button Uses

1. It is used to power (that is, to "On") your iPhone when it is clicked.

2. When you press and hold the Up Volume and Power buttons it will launch the Switch Off slider, Medical ID slider, and Emergency slider page or activate the emergency call.

3. It could be used to call Siri when you press and hold the button.

4. It could be used to bring it to sleep condition and to reawaken it.

5. It could be used to take *Screenshots* by pressing down both the up volume button and power button at the same time.

Silence Button: The button is located at the top left side of the iPhone. It is the first button. This is a sliding button that must be either push backward to activate silence mode or pull forward to deactivate silence mode.

Silence Button Uses

It is used to silence messages, notifications,

and ring hepatic sounds. When calls enter, you would not hear the ringing tone or sound, if the button has been activated by pushing it backward.

Up Volume Button: This is the second button at the top left of the iPhone.

Silence Button Uses
1. It is used to increase the volume of a sound on your iPhone.
2. It is used to take Photos when the Camera app is open by clicking the button instead of tapping on the shutter.
3. It is used to force the shutdown of the iPhone when it is pressed together with the down volume and power button.

Down Volume Button: This is the third button at the top left of the iPhone.

Silence Button Uses
1. It is used to decrease the volume of a sound on your iPhone.
2. It is used to take Photos when the Camera app is open by clicking the button instead of tapping on the shutter.
3. It is used to force the shutdown of the iPhone when it is pressed together with the up volume and power button.

CHAPTER ONE

How You Could Solve Problems on iOS 14 Features

In this iPhone 12, Mini, Pro & Max manual, easy methods to solve problems are introduced. It is so simple for dummies and beginners to follow and understand without making any mistake in providing solutions to your ways of operating the iPhone perfectly.

You are given a large clear opportunity of knowing what to do at the starting point to the ending point by telling you where to start; where to end your search and how to return to the starting page.

Although, several authors preferred writing operational steps in what I called "**Condensed format**". For instance, if you want to enable **Live Photo** on your iPhone in a Condensed format, it will be written as **Settings < Camera < Preserving Settings <** Switch On **Live Photo.**

As a beginner, this method will be difficult for you to get your problem solved because the steps did not explain how you will locate your target on each page.

But, in this manual, all the operational techniques were fully explained.

The name of the page at which you could find what you are looking for is written in bold red font size e.g. Settings, Camera, Siri, Customized Control…etc.

Let's convert the above Condensed format steps to my *Comprehensive Steps* to activate **Live Photo** on your iPhone**.**

Homescreen: Hit on the **Settings App** icon (first line of action)

Settings: Scroll down and hit on the **Camera** icon (Second line of action)

Camera: Select **Preserving Settings** (Third line of action)

Preserve Settings: Hit on the **Live Photo's** activation switch to change from white ⚪ to green. 🟢

On the *first line of action*, you will see Homescreen appears in a bold red color font size which means the **page name**, while **Settings App** appears in a bold black font means "what you are looking for on the page (i.e. *your mission*)".

On the *second line of action*, the **Settings App** changes to Settings because at this stage you have launched the Settings page and on the page, you will see **Settings** at the top of the page therefore the bold red color look of the Settings is telling you that you are now in the Settings page, *not mission*, while **Camera** is your next mission on the Settings page.

On the *third line of action* the bold black font **Camera** changed to bold red font Camera, this is to tell you that you are now on the Camera Page and you will be looking for **Preserving Settings...** and when you hit on it you will see **Live Photo** to activate and the Preserving Settings will become the name of the page.

Meaning of Common Terms (Words)

Please get used to the meaning of the below simple terms I used in this book to help rapid learning and digestion of different technical steps.

Hit or **Select**: This means **"Tap"**. Whenever you see "hit" on a particular **application** or **feature**, I mean you should tap on the app or the feature.

Activator: It is used for the "switch button" to turn on apps features in Settings. ⚪ or 🟢

Activate: This means you should turn on the **Activator.** ⚪

Deactivate: This means you should turn off the **Activator.** ⚪

Regulator: It means **"Control"**. It has a round button on a parallel line that can be moved to either right or left to regulate the level of volume of a sound or light on your iPhone Settings.

Type: It means "Enter" words or numbers into a text or searches field.

Text or Search Field: This is a place where you can type in words or numbers

How to Use all the Functional Icons on Lock Screen

The Importance of Applications (Apps)

The applications (Apps) features on your iPhone 12, Mini, Pro, or Max are designed to perform different functions. As the name implies "Application", is a tool you could easily apply to perform all you want on your iPhone.

Let's consider the Camera App, for instance, you can frequently use Camera Application to do the following; recording videos, taking photos, and editing photos to be used for documentation or media presentation and future purposes.

Camera App has lightning effect tools and filter that contain different sub-tools or equipment that could enable you to add beautiful effects to all saved recorded videos, photos and consequently make them come out pretty good for Personal Photo, Profile Picture, Wallpaper, Media Presentation, or Video Watch… and many others.

Therefore, you could quickly know all the available apps on your iPhone 12, Mini, Pro, or Max Apps through the different **Icons** that represented them. When you tap on their Icons and you will access all the feature functions inside the apps. ***Camera App is represented with Camera Image as Icon.***

How Apps Works

By default, several App will be automatically installed after the setup; however, before you can benefit from all the advanced features on your iPhone you will need to enable their activation switches in the **Settings App**.

This will be fully discussed later in this iPhone 12, Mini, Pro, or Max Manual.

What are the Icons on iPhone 12, Mini, Pro, or Max Screens?

The major screens of your iPhone are:

1. **Lock Screen**
2. **Home Screen**

iOS 14 Lock Screen

This is the first-page screen that contains a timer, date, notifications, camera icon, cellular icon, Wi-Fi network icon, battery icon, flash icon, and security lock icon.

The most important features of the icons on the Lock screen are:

Cellular Icon: The icon is showing the level of network service on your iPhone. The three inclined vertical bars show the strength of the network on your iPhone wherever you are.

LTE: When you see LTE on your iPhone 12, Mini, Pro, or Max top this shows that at the location you are there is a strong network that can make your activity on the internet to be very faster on your 3G and 4G iPhone.

26

5G: Your iPhone is designed to use 5G SIM and lower-G SIM cellular networks. The 5G network is the fastest cellular network.

Wi-Fi: This is an internet browsing network that makes use of data to upload, download, update, or transfer documents; and to connect Android, Apple Watch, or iPhone to your iPhone 12, Mini, Pro, or Max. The Icon can be found beside the cellular icon at the top right of the iPhone. You will read more later in this Manual.

Battery Icon: This is showing the level of battery charged on your iPhone. If the battery is going down the level of the battery will be reduced from the right end to the left end of the battery. The icon is at the top right of the iPhone. You will read more later.

Lock Icon: When the Padlock is open it shows that the iPhone is open but when it remains locked that means that the Lock Screen is still locked.

Timer: It automatically set itself with the most accurate regional global time of your location. It instantly determines regional timing.

Notifications: You can only see the notification on the Lock screen, if you have activated it in the Setting app that alert notification should be shown on the lock screen.

You further set climatic weather/temperature widget, missed calls, alarm, received emails, messages notification. However, you may avoid your messages or mail details from showing on the Lock screen through notification settings; to prevent anyone from viewing your privacy.

You have to unlock your iPhone before you can perform the following:

Flash: You can use the flash at the bottom left of the Lock screen to lightening the dark environment and facilitates sharp and clear output of pictures taking in uniformly dark surroundings.

Camera: It can be constantly used to perform video coverage, and pictures taking without you navigating through the Homescreen.

Also, you could swipe from the right side of the iPhone to launch the Camera page or press the Switch button to access Camera and click on any of the **down or up volume** buttons at the left side of the iPhone to take a picture if you don't want to use Shutter at the bottom center of the Camera screen.

Searching Page: When you slide your iPhone from the left side of the screen, you will see searching tools that will enable you to find many apps information on your iPhone. Ask more of Apple store, iCloud, or Siri to know more about them. There is much informative news that is displayed below that you can hit on to read more if your Wi-Fi network is On.

Place your finger at the bottom center of the Notch base of your iPhone and slightly move down your finger you will see a searching field with suggested favorite Apps that you can navigate to get what you need on the iPhone.

But, if that app you are looking for is not among the suggested apps, you can further type in the app into the searching field to access the app.

Hint: Anytime you see **Search or Text Field** in a page without seeing Keyboard below to type text into the field. All you need to do is to first and foremost hit on the surface of the **Search or Text field**, and instantly the Keyboard will appear below the field in the page for you to enter your search text keywords into the field. Examples of apps that contain text fields are Homescreen Apps Library Search Field, Mail, Messages, Safari, or other Browsers, Camera, Call Contact, Calendar, FaceTime, Health... and many others.

Control Center: For you to access Control Center from the Lock screen, you have to unlock the screen with the security on your iPhone. The security may be Face ID or Password; however, it depends on the security you registered during the iPhone setup.

When you swipe down from the right side of the lock screen, the Control center will slide down to show all the available default and customized apps controls.

If you use Face ID for your security, the Lock screen will be unlocked immediately after the Infrared blinking light from the iPhone Notch scans your face.

How to know all the Functions of all the Applications and Their Icons in Homescreen

You could completely do everything that you do on the Lock screen on the Homescreen; even more, can be done directly.

You can repeat the side screen and the Notch frame center searching methods on the Homescreen. Alternatively, swipe left from the left side of the iPhone repeatedly till you get to the third page of Apps Libraries to search for apps you are looking for.

Several icons are available for you to navigate on to ease your smooth findings and operational functions. The individual app name is mentioned below as they were arranged row by row in the Homepage picture above.

This is the list of various applications

(apps) that are available on your iPhone running by iOS 14 are
Messages, 9 *Calendar,* *Photos,* *Camera,* *Weather,* *Clock,* *Maps,* *FaceTime,* *Notes,* *Reminder,* *Stocks,* *News,* *Home,* *iTune Store,* *Apple Store,* *Books,* *Health,* *Wallet,* *Settings,* *Podcast,* *Phone,* *Mail,* *Safari,* *Music,* *Find My,* *Shortcuts,* *Contacts,* *Compass,* *Measure,* *Calculator,* *Files,* *Watch, and* *Tips.*

You can still request more apps on your iPhone through Apple Store freely. More apps you can get from the Apple store are *iMovie, iTunes Remote, iTunes U, Number, GarageBand, Clips, Keynote, Pages, and Music Memos.*

All the above apps are very important for you to fully benefit the operational efficiency of your iPhone and make life very simple to explore and achievable. **The most important and inevitable Apps that you must know the beneficial features are: Settings, Call, Messages, Camera, Photo, FaceTime, Siri, Safari, Mail, and Music.**

Settings: This app will enable you to access the settings of all the available apps on your iPhone. Through the Settings app, you can perfectly activate all the essential apps (e.g. Face ID, Siri, Passcode, Wi-Fi Network, iCloud, etc.) that you are unable or skipped during your iPhone setup.

Phone: This will enable you to reach out to your friends or loved ones that you are having their **contact** details on your iPhone. The phone app will enable you to receive and make a call.

Massage: This will enable you to send text messages to your loved ones in your contacts. You have two ways of sending a message to people.

1. SMS or MMS

2. iMessage

SMS or MMS: You can send a text message through SMS and MMS to anyone on your contact that is using an Android phone. The sending button is green

iMessage: This is a live interactive message medium that will enable you to see when the person you are sending your text message to is typing his/her messages. It is only available for those who are using an iPhone. The sending icon is blue.

Camera: This will enable you to take new pictures or images and record videos of any event. In it, there is image beatifying features that can be applied to edit and modify the image output.

Photos: In this app, you can fully access all your saved pictures regarding time, day, month, location, and event. This app will arrange and indicate the source of store images such as *Screenshot, WhatsApp, Facebook, Video, Movies, DCIM, Camera, Live Pictures...and others.* You can add labels to any specific event photographs.

FaceTime: As the name of the app implies **FaceTime,** it will enable you to make face to face calls, audio calls, live to chat text messages on your iPhone with the use of the latest Animoji or customized, Memoji and Emoji.

Siri: This app is a wonderful work-executor and apps, problem solver. It serves as a messenger or personal assistant to help you determine several activities associated with other apps on your iPhone. It can help

you set and save time in Alarm, a reminder for events, check daily weather/climatic condition, recall the missed calls or messages and it can also help you compose messages and send to whosoever you want to send it to.

If you call its attention, it will do anything you want it to do for you. Its voice could be set to female or male voice all depends on your choice. It is one of the great successes ever apple has achieved in using technology to solve the iPhone user's bothering issues with ease.

How to talk to Siri

Safari: This app is used to browse for any information online or to download more applications, games, dictionaries, music, videos, language translator, WhatsApp, Facebook… and many others.

Mail: The App will enable you to instantly access your received email messages and to reply to messages.

Music: This app will enable you to play any audio music in your music library.

Health: This is an amazing app that you can use to track everything about your health to ensure your daily general wellbeing. You can also use it to monitor your daily food consumption through the regulation of calories and monthly menstrual cycle in women; heart condition, fasting discipline, sleeping status, working ability… and many other activities essential to your comfortable life.

Find My: This is App very important to either quickly use to locate your misplaced iPhone or retrieve a suspected lost iPhone without using a Wi-Fi network or Cellular connection even when the battery is done you can still recover your lost iPhone.

By now you must have prepared to practically use all the basic and essential apps on your iPhone.

Many apps features were discussed in this perfect guide which will help you on how to effectively use your newly purchased iPhone 12 mini, iPhone 12, iPhone 12 Pro, or iPhone 12 Pro Max.

Now let's move to the next level of practical iPhone operation.

CHAPTER TWO

How to Make Your iPhone Start Working

Get your iPhone on your hand and start this step by step method of bringing out the beauty of your iPhone to start enjoying the super-benefits of the iPhone.

The Location of Dual SIM Tray on iPhone 12, Mini, Pro, and Max

Although, most of the time dual SIM Tray compartment is positioned at the either middle or lower right side of the previous iPhones, however, the location of the dual SIM Tray on the newly released iPhones is positioned at the lower left side of the iPhone.

Step 1: Let your iPhone screen faces up as it was shown in the picture above.

Step 2: Put the pointed end of the *SIM Tray Ejector* inside the *SIM Tray Hole* and ensure it touches the internal surface.

Step 3: Push the surface inward and the SIM Tray will instantly come out.

Step 4: Use your hand to completely remove the SIM Tray from the compartment.

The SIM Tray has up and down faced that you can fix your SIM. If you are using nano-SIM you will fix it under and if you are using eSIM you will fix it at the upper face.

The nano-SIM-designed tray side has a support that will prevent nano-SIM from falling when you turn the SIM Tray upside down, while the eSIM tray side has no support, therefore, if you mistakenly turn it the other way round the eSIM will fall instantly.

Before you place the nano-SIM inside its tray side, look at the designed shape on the tray, and ensure that the metal surface faces up not down. Also for eSIM; let the metal surface faces up.

To properly guide you, in the picture below I drew a noticeable line around the border of the nano-SIM tray and eSIM to know you will position the SIM

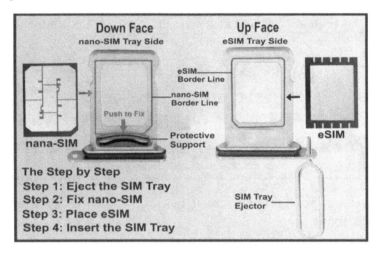

Step 5: Insert the SIM tray inside the SIM compartment the same way you remove it as it was shown in the picture above.

Ensure the SIM tray is completely inserted to have the SIM tray cover leveled with the side body of the iPhone. More so, if you are only having one of the compatible SIM, you can fix it on its tray and insert the tray.

Now let's move to the next stage of having your iPhone start working.

How to Setup your iPhone Manually after Purchase

The manual setup of your iPhone is as simple as you reading alphabet a, b, c..., if you completely make all the necessary things available and strictly follow the setup step by step one after the other.

What You Must Do First
1. Ensure that your iPhone is fully charged. If you are having a fully charged computer, you can connect the iPhone USB cable to your iPhone power port and the computer USB port to charge it.
2. If you are having any data to transfer from Android, old iPhone, or Computer, turn on the Wi-Fi Network of the old iPhone or Computer.
3. You can name the Wi-Fi for easy recognition on your new iPhone.
4. Make sure that the Wi-Fi network is very active and strong.

Better still, you could do the data or document transfer after the manual setup because the transfer of data can be more successful if you use the Wi-Fi of the new iPhone. The process of performing data and document transfer from other devices would be discussed later.

The Manual Setup Step by Step
1. Power Switch Button
   Look at the right side of the new iPhone you will see a button, Press down till you will see a big **Hello** font interpreting in different languages on the screen

2. Hello
   Swipe up from the bottom center to tap on your **Language**.

3. Select Your Country or Region
   Scroll down to tap on your **Country.**

4. **Quick Start**
   Look down the screen hit on **Set Up Manually.**

5. **Choose a Wi-Fi Network**
   Hit on the name of your **Wi-Fi Source.**

6. **Enter Password**
   Enter the correct password of the **Wi-Fi Network** and tap on **Join** at the top right side of the screen.

7. **Data & Privacy**
   Hit the **Continue** bar

8. **Face ID**
   a. Hit on the **Continue** bar.
   b. Hit on the **"Get Started"** bar
   c. Focus your eyes on the Front-Facing Camera Sensor and let your head be in the middle of the round frame on the screen.
   d. As you are turning your head gradually the surrounding lines of the round frame will be changing to green, keep turning your head and let every side of your head be captured by the Camera sensor

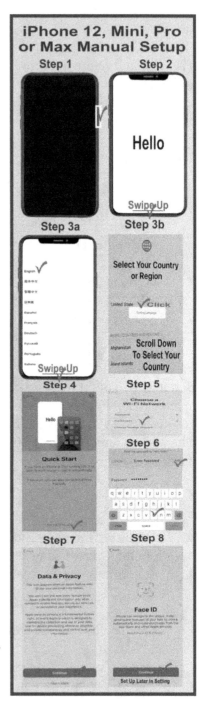

36

till the surrounding lines are completely changed to green.

e. If the Face ID is successful, a **Continue** page will display. Hit the **Continue** bar.

9. For later Face ID Settings hit the second option **Set Up Later in Settings.**

10. Create a Passcode
Use the Keypad to type a complex **Passcode.** But, if you are not prepared, then tap on **Passcode Options** and hit on **Don't Use Passcode.**

11. Passcode Box
Hit on **Don't Use Passcode.**

12. Apps & Data
If you are having data on Android Phone you can hit on the option **Move Data from Android. Other options**

a. Restore from iCloud Backup

b. Restore from Mac or PC

c. Don't Transfer Apps & Data

13. Apple ID

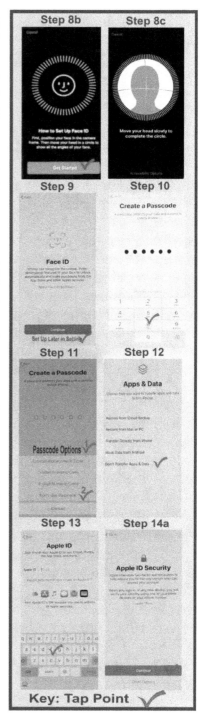

37

a. Tap on the Text Field, use the Keyboard to type your Email address

b. Hit on **Next** at the top right angle side.

c. Type a correct **Apple Password** inside the text field.

d. Hit on **Next** at the top right angle side.

14. Apple ID Security

Hit the **Continue** bar to register your **Phone Number.**

But, if do not want that to be done during setup then you tap on **Other Options** Hit on **Don't Upgrade** on the **Request Box.**

15. Terms and Condition

Read through the terms and conditions that are required of you on how to successfully use your iPhone and follow them strictly. Tap on the **Agree** option at the downright area of the screen.

16. Express Settings

Hit **Continue** bar below

17. Keep Your iPhone Up to Date

Choose the below option

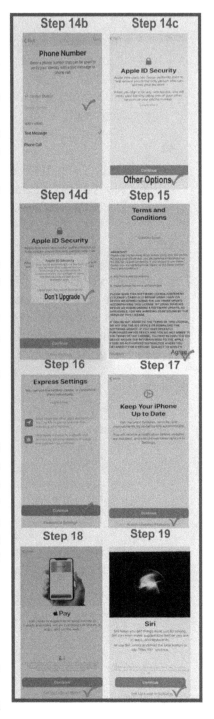

of **Install Update Manually.**

18. Apple Pay

Enter your Apple Wallet detail if it is available with you by hitting on the **Continue** bar.

But, choose **Set Up Later in the Wallet** option below, if you don't have one.

19. Siri

Tap on the **Continue** bar to register Siri (optional)

But, tap on **Set Up Later in Settings** to perform the full settings of Siri through the Settings process.

20. Screen Timer

Hit **Continue** bar (optional), it could be done later, therefore, for now, choose **Set Up Later in Settings.**

21. Apple Analytics

Select the **Don't Share** option below Share with App Developers.

22. True Tone Display

Hit on the **Continue** bar

23. Appearance

a. Select on the **Light** option to make the

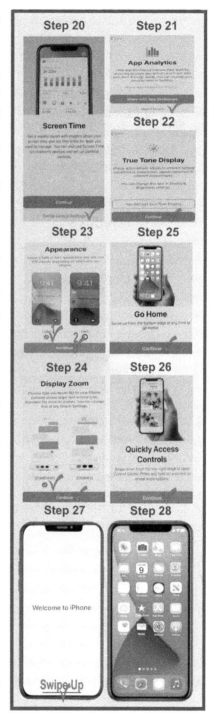

39

iPhone screen appear brighter.
b. Hit **Continue** bar

24. Display Zoom
Hit **Standard** small circle to select it.
Hit **Continue** bar

25. Go Home
Hit **Continue** bar

26. Switch Between Recent Apps
Hit **Continue** bar

27. Quickly Access Controls
Hit **Continue** bar

28. Welcome to iPhone
Swipe up from the bottom middle of the screen to access the **Homepage.** If you create a Passcode during setup, the iPhone will ask you to enter your registered Passcode before you can launch into the Homescreen.

Currently, you can use your iPhone to make a call, text message, and do all you want to do. But if do not know how to go about that, everything is discussed in this manual to help. Go through the other guides' sections to get the facts you are looking for.

As I have promised that you would fully learn details on how you can easily transfer data or documents from your old iPhone, Android phone, Computer, or any gadget to your newly purchased iPhone.

The next stage is how you could transfer data or documents to your iPhone if you do have any important documents to move from old gadgets to the new iPhone.

Note: Your documents may include music files, photo, video files, messages files… and many others.

How You Could Transfer Data or Documents from Any Gadget to Your New iPhone

What You Should Do First on Old iPhone
1. You have to ensure that the old iPhone iOS is upgraded to iOS 11 and above.
2. Backup the data or documents with PC or Mac.
3. Recharge the iPhone Battery to be fully charged.
4. Turn On the Cellular connection and Wi-Fi network.
5. Turn On "Find My iPhone" in Setting.
6. Write the correct Apple ID into a planner or notebook.

How You Could Turn On Hotspot and Enter Wi-Fi Password on Old iPhone

 In this manual, I will be transferring data from the iPhone X that is running with iOS 11 into any of the latest iPhones (i.e., iPhone 12, Mini, Pro, and Max).

You will have to take a little proactive step to enable Hotspot through the Settings App on your old iPhone.

First Step:

➢ Swipe down the top right side of the old iPhone to launch Control Center.

➢ Tap on the Wi-Fi icon and Bluetooth icon to enable them.

In a situation whereby the Wi-Fi is unable to activate or not functioning, then take the following steps to enable *Personal Hotspot* from the settings.

On the Homescreen: Tap on **Settings Button**

Settings Page: Tap on **Personal Hotspot**

Hotspot Page:

1. Tap on **Personal Hotspot** activation switch to turn green.

2. On the dialog box, Wi-Fi and Bluetooth are Off, then tap on **Turn On Wi-Fi and Bluetooth.**

3. On displayed Bluetooth Off Dialog Box tap on **Wi-Fi and USB Only.**

4. Tap on **Wi-Fi Password**

Wi-Fi Password:

1. Tap on the **Password Text Field surface** and use the keyboard below on the page to enter your "**Wi-Fi Password**".

2. Tap on **Done** at the top angle of the iPhone.

3. Tap on the Home button to return to Homescreen. But, if your old iPhone is iPhone X above then swipe up from the bottom center to go back to the Homescreen.

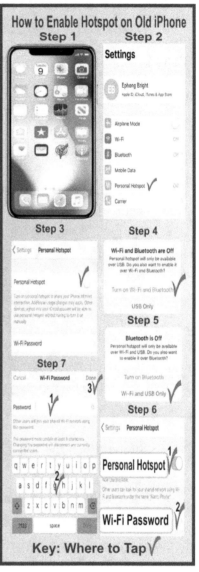

Now that the old iPhone Wi-Fi Network, Cellular Service, and Bluetooth were turned on and active, you can move to the next stage of transferring data from the old iPhone to your new iPhone 12, Mini, Pro, or Max.

The Step by Step for Automatic Data Transfer from Old iPhone to New iPhone

How to Position the Old iPhone and New iPhone

Position the two iPhones side by side as they were shown in the picture. There should be a 3cm distance between the old iPhone and the new iPhone. Let there be no much distance between them to enable the quick signal connection between both iPhones.

You can either place the old iPhone on your left-hand side or otherwise. If you will be more convenient with the right positioning of the new iPhone due to the fact that you are a right-hand user, then let your new iPhone be placed at the right-hand side.

But, if the left side is easier for you, then you could rather position the new iPhone to the left-hand side. What is important for you is to choose a more convenient side for the new iPhone because you will do more activities on the new iPhone than the old one.

If you must carry any of the iPhone to enter Password or do anything, you must make sure you keep to the recommended 3cm distance between them when you put it down. It is very important.

What You Must Do First on Your New iPhone 12, Mini, Pro, or Max
- ➢ Ensure that the iPhone battery is fully charged.
- ➢ You have to confirm the total storage space used by the data or documents on the old iPhone and the available storage space on the new iPhone if it will be enough to accept the data or documents you wanted to transfer.

To confirm the Storage Space on your new iPhone

- Homescreen: Hit on **Settings** Icon.
- Settings: At the top hit on **Sign In to Your iPhone** or **Your Name** beside your Profile Picture.
- Apple ID: Tap on **iCloud**
- iCloud: At the top, you will see the number of storage used and the storage remain. (*If you do not have enough you may buy more storage from iCloud*).

➢ Go to **Control Center** to tap on Wi-Fi, Bluetooth, and Cellular network.

➢ Rename your Wi-Fi network for quick recognition on another device (optional).

➢ Make sure there is a strong network on your iPhone.

Start the Automatic Set Up for the New iPhone

1. Positioning

➢ Place both old and new iPhone beside each other on a table.

2. Old iPhone

➢ Unlock the old iPhone and let it be on Homescreen.

3. New iPhone

➢ Press the switch button to "On" the new iPhone.

➢ Swipe up Hello, within a second your new iPhone will be seen on the screen of the old iPhone.

4. Set Up New iPhone **(Old iPhone)**

➢ Under the new iPhone's image hit the **Continue** bar.

➢ Within a second a round white shape Camera space will show up for you to capture the moving circular eruption on the new iPhone.

➢ Take the old iPhone above the new iPhone, let the rear Camera focus on the moving circular eruption, to be viewed in the center of the round Viewfinder space on the old iPhone above.

➢ Hold on till you will see "**Finish on New iPhone**" on the old iPhone before you will return it to its formal position.

While the old iPhone is transferring the information into the new iPhone then go to the **new iPhone** to continue.

5. Enter Passcode of Old iPhone (**New iPhone**)
   ➢ Type the Passcode of your old iPhone without making a mistake. Setting Up Your iPhone will show on the screen. Wait till you will see Face ID.
6. Face ID
   ➢ Hit on the **Continue** bar.
   ➢ Hit on the "**Get Started**" bar
   ➢ Focus your eyes on the Front-Facing Camera Sensor and let your head be in the middle of the round Viewfinder frame on the screen.
   ➢ As you are turning your head gradually the surrounding lines of the round frame will be changing to green, keep turning your head and let every side of your head be captured by the Camera sensor till the surrounding lines are completely changed to green.
   ➢ If the first Face ID scanner is successful, hit on the **Continue** bar and

Automatic Setup & Data Transfer
Step 1
Press the Power Button to Switch On
Step 2 & 3
Hello
Swipe Up Step 2
Swipe Up Step 3
Step 4a
Let Rear Camera Focusing for iPhone...
Step 4b
Waiting for Other iPhone...
Step 5
Enter Passcode of Your Other iPhone
Step 6a
Face ID
Key: Where to Tap

45

move your head in either the same or opposite way, once the second Face ID scanner is complete another page will show and tell you that "**Face ID is Now Set-Up**"

➢ Hit on the **Continue** bar

7. Face ID (If you do not want Face ID for now)

➢ For "later Face ID Settings" hit the second option **Set Up Later in Settings.**

8. Transfer Your Data

➢ Tap on **Transfer from iPhone.** If you have updated all your apps and data, you are good to go.

➢ You may also choose **Transfer from iCloud** if you are very sure that it is up to date. You may tap on **Other Options** to select any other device like Android, Mac, PC, etc.

9. Terms and Condition

Read and digest the terms and conditions for you to know how you could successfully use your iPhone and follow them strictly. Tap on the **Agree** option at the bottom right of the screen.

10. Settings From Other iPhone

➢ Hit on the **Continue** bar to proceed.

11. **Keep Your iPhone Up to Date**
➢ Choose the below option of **Install Update Manually.**
12. **Apple Pay**
Enter your Apple Wallet detail if it is available to you by tapping on the **Continue** bar.
But, choose the "**Set Up Later in Wallet**" option below if you don't have one.
13. **Apple Watch**
➢ Tap on **Set Up Later** under the continue bar to proceed.

14. **Apple Analytics**
Select the **Don't Share** option below Share with App Developers. The next interface will show you how the data is moving from your old iPhone to the new iPhone.
15. **Old iPhone**

When all the data are completely moved into your new iPhone 12, Mini, Pro, and Max, it will show on the screen of the old iPhone that "**Transfer Complete**".

Hit on the **Continue** bar to enter the Homescreen of your old iPhone.

16. **New iPhone**

The New iPhone will show Apple's

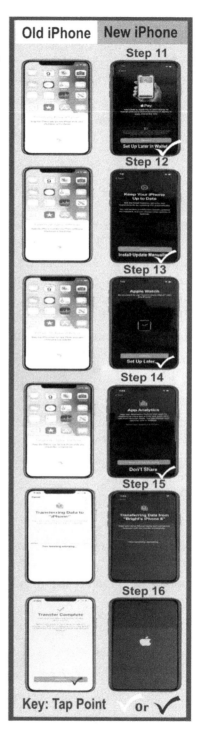

47

image on the screen. After a while, it will change the screen face to a white interface. Swipe Up the screen from the bottom center and launch into the data loading with the Apple image interface on the new iPhone 12, Mini, Pro, and Max.

You have to endure enough to allow all the data and apps to absolutely moving from old iPhone to new iPhone because the uncompleted Apps will appear black with a faded icon image on the Homescreen. You will only see the icons that are completely loaded on your screen as they have appeared on your old iPhone.

Hint: You can also transfer the latest data, and apps from the newly set up iPhone 12, Mini, Pro, or Max to iPhone X and above to upgrade and have the same look; and functions of iPhone 12, Mini, Pro, and Max.

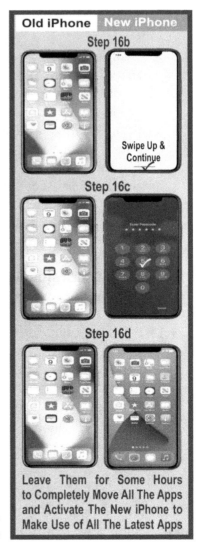

The other method of sending images or screenshots from Safari to another iPhone device by using AirDrop will be discussed later under the general use of Safari App.

How You Can Successfully Send Data, Video, or Photo Files from Android Phone to Your iPhone

This is very helpful to all beginners or dummies that are worried about transferring their valuable data, documents, or files like video, audio, and photos, etc. to their newly purchased iPhone 12, Mini, Pro, or Max.

These are the important things you initially do on your Android phone before starting the documents transfer:

- ✓ You should make sure that your Android Phone Battery and iPhone Battery are 100% charged.
- ✓ Use a strong Wi-Fi Network and turn On your Bluetooth. Alternatively, you can initially do the **manual setup** of the new iPhone for you to use the new iPhone Hotspot Wi-Fi Connection on your Android to fast track the data or document transfer.

Take these steps on your old Android Phone

Homescreen

➢ Hit on Google Play Icon.

Google Play

➢ Hit on the text field of Google Play at the top of the page
➢ Use Keyboard to enter **Move to iOS** and tap on the suggested **Move to iOS** keyword dropdown.

Move to 1OS

Hit on the **Open** bar

➢ Do not hit on **Continue** until you are on the page of Apps & Data where you will first hit on **Move Data from Android**

49

On your iPhone 12, Mini, Pro, or Max

1. Click the **Power button** on the right side of the iPhone.
2. Swipe Up the **Hello** page from the bottom and select your **language** (e.g. English**).**

Select Your Country or Region

1. Scroll down to select your Country by tapping on it.
2. Allow it to complete the **Setting Language…** processing.

Quick Start: Hit on **Set Up Manually.**

Choose a Wi-Fi Network: Select the exact **Wi-Fi network** you are using.

Enter Password:

1. Type the **"Password" for the Wi-Fi** correctly into the **Password Text Field.**
2. Hit on **Join** at the top right of the page.

50

Data and Privacy: Hit on **Continue Bar**

Face ID: Hit on **Set Up Later in Settings.** If you have not done the Face ID.

Create Passcode:

1. Hit on **Passcode Options** and select on a dialog box **Don't Use Passcode**. It is optional, you may create the Passcode if you want to.
2. On another dialog box showing that "**Using a Passcode is Highly Recommended**" select "**Don't Use Passcode**" again to continue.

Apps & Data: Hit on **Move Data from Android.**

➡ iOS Move from Android

➢ Hit on **Continue** below
➢ Type the "**Code**" that shows on the screen of your iPhone into your Android phone.

On Android Phone

Move to iOS

➢ Hit on **Continue** above the iOS phone image.

Terms and Conditions

➢ Hit on **Agree**

51

Find Your Code

> ➢ Hit on **Next** at the top angle of the screen.

Enter Code

> ➢ Use the Keypad to enter the **Code** on the iPhone into your Android Phone.

Transfer Data:

> ➢ Select all the documents or data that you wanted to send from your Android to your new iPhone.
> ➢ Hit on **Next** at the top corner of the screen.

If you do not tap on **Next** at the top right of the Android phone your iPhone will keep waiting for you to complete the command.

Hint: Do not switch to other apps or turn off the android phone until the transfer is complete.

Ensure you position your Android phone very close to your iPhone.

52

If you have taken too much time before you enter the code into your Android Phone the transfer may be impossible.

If you experienced an unsuccessful transfer, immediately, hit **Back** at the top left of the iPhone screen and re-tap on **Continue** to get another code. Enter the code fast into your Android Phone.

As soon as the transfer is complete on your new iPhone then tap on **Continue Setting Up iPhone.**

Continue your iPhone setup steps from Step 13 above under manual setup or step 9 under automatic setup to complete the iPhone setup.

Simple Ways of Upgrading Old iPhones to Latest iOS 14

This will enable you to upgrade your second-generation old iPhones which include iPhone X, XR, XS, XS Max, 11, 11 Pro, 11 Pro Max, and SE 2020.

When the iPhone is upgraded you could also befit all the innovative functions in iPhone 12 Mini, 12, 12 Pro, and 12 Pro Max which include the adding of Widget on Homepage, having latest wallpaper, smart app navigation, improved super-speed download provided you have enough storage space (memory), professional camera coverage and photo editing... and many others.

Things You Must Put In Place Before You Start
- ➢ Get an effective Wi-Fi network.
- ➢ Confirm the available storage space on your iPhone. If you do not have up to 90 GB you can purchase from the iCloud store for more storage.
- ➢ Use iCloud or Mac or PC to back up all the data and documents on your iPhone.

- ➢ Charge your iPhone, and Mac or PC. You may connect your iPhone or upgrading device to a power source overnight.
- ➢ Make your Password available.
- ➢ Good lightning to USB cord.

How to perform Backup and iOS Upgrade on Computer

The Operational System for Apple Macintosh Computer (Mac)

- ➢ macOS Catalina 10.15 or
- ➢ macOS Mojave 10.14 or lower version.

Note: You may use a PC if you do not have Mac.

If your Mac is running with a low version of macOS Mojave you can quickly update your Mac by taking the following step on your Mac.

On App Menu:

- ➢ Select **System Preferences** (operating system).
- ➢ Click on **Software Update** to look for an Updates
- ➢ Click on the **Update Now** option to install the

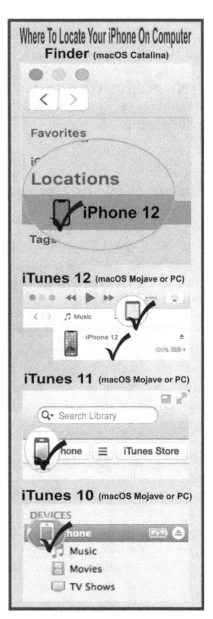

Where To Locate Your iPhone On Computer
Finder (macOS Catalina)

Favorites

Locations

iPhone 12

Tags

iTunes 12 (macOS Mojave or PC)

♫ Music

iPhone 12

100%

iTunes 11 (macOS Mojave or PC)

Search Library

hone ≡ iTunes Store

iTunes 10 (macOS Mojave or PC)

DEVICES

hone

♫ Music

Movies

TV Shows

54

latest version benefits. If you select **More Info** you will see full information on the individual update and later choose the one you preferred.

➤ Leave it for a while to completely install till you will see a message that "**your software is up to date**.

Now you can confidently move on to the update process of your iPhone on your newly updated Mac.

Step by Step of iPhone Update on macOS Catalina 10.15

➤ Put On your Mac.
➤ Put On the Wi-Fi network connection on your Mac or PC

➤ Launch **Finder**

But if you are using a Mac running with macOS Mojave 10.14 or less, you will open **iTunes**

Step by Step of iPhone Update on macOS Catalina 10.15

➤ Use the lightning to USB Cable to connect your iPhone with the Mac USB port.

➤ Look at the left side of the Finder page you will see the image of your iPhone and the iPhone name under **Location.**

- (If you have signed up your name with Apple ID, your first name will appear at the front of the iPhone image). Hit on the name of your iPhone.

- The location at which you can locate your iPhone differs from the iTunes version to another iTunes version in macOS Mojave and PC.

- However, the location of your iPhone on iTunes 10 – 12 was shown on the screenshot below.

➤ Once you click on your iPhone the Update provisional page for your iPhone will display on the right-hand side.

➤ Initially click on **Backup all the data on your iPhone to this Mac.**

➤ Click **Check for Update.**

- ➤ Click **Download** and **Update.**
- ➤ When you are asked to provide your **Passcode,** immediately type your **Passcode.**
  The update will start, endure until the update is complete.
  Do not interrupt the update processing.

How to perform iOS Update on your New iPhone

Homescreen:

- ➤ Place your finger at the top right of the iPhone screen and swipe down to launch **Control Center.**
- ➤ Hit on Cellular Service ⬭ and Wi-Fi network. 📶
- ➤ Swipe up from the bottom or hit the down plain of the screen to return to Homescreen.
- ➤ Hit on **Settings Icon.** ⚙

Settings: Scroll down to hit on **General**

General: Hit on **Software Update.**

Software Update: Select **Download** and **Install**

If your passcode is required then continue by:

Passcode: Type the correct **Passcode.**

Terms and Conditions: Select **Agree** at the lower left to progress but if you mistakenly select **Disagree** it will discontinue the upgrade.

Immediately, the Upgrade will start, and you can let the iPhone upgrade overnight to finish the general processing because it always takes much time.

CHAPTER THREE

How You Could Add Widgets on Your Homepage and Searching Page

For the sake of the beginners and dummies, the Searching page could be found on your iPhone when you swipe right from your main Homepage (i.e. swipe homepage from the left side of the screen toward the right side).

At this time, I will completely take you through the unique innovativeness in your newly purchased iPhone running with iOS 14. One of the special features in this iOS 14 is the ability you have to customize the Homescreen by adding Widgets including Siri Suggestions, Weather, Clock, Notes, News, Stocks, Photos, Reminders, Maps, Music, Apple TV, Screen Time, Recent Noted, Tips (about what's new in iOS 14) ... and many others.

The widget could be automatically rotated to show the most accurate information throughout the day which could be scrolled through conveniently.

Step By Step of How to Add Widgets

Home Screen:

- ➢ On the Home screen press down and hold for 2 seconds till you will see the entire Apps' Icons shaking and carry **Remove Sign (-)** in a white circle at the top left side of each App on the Homescreen.
- ➢ At the top left of the Home screen where you normally see Digital **Time,** you will see **Add Sign (+),** tap on **Add.**

Widget Page

- ➢ **Use Search Field**: You will see a Searching Field at the top. Hit the field to enter the name of the Widget you want. For example, type in **Weather** for a daily weather forecast. Hit on **Search** blue button at the bottom right of the

57

keyboard, or tap on the weather image display below the search field to enter and search immediately.

➤ **Without Using Search Field:** once you open the Widget page, scroll down till you will see the Weather Widget. Hit it to select the widget.

➤ You will see different sizes of Widget like small size, medium, and large size. If you want the smallest size, it will occupy the space of 4 Apps' Icons on the Home screen; medium smart stack that will occupy the space of 8 Apps' Icons on the Home screen, while the biggest smart stack widget will occupy 20 icons' space on the Homescreen.

➤ To start with, select the Medium Smart Stack.

➤ Hit on the **Add Widget** button below.

Home Screen:

➤ If you want to move the Weather Widget around the page you could just use your finger to press and move the widget to anywhere you prefer.

➤ When you are satisfied with the position on your screen then tap on **Done** at the top right side of the screen.

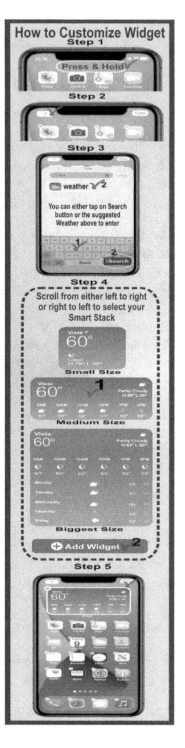

58

Note: The Mark/Check sign ✔ *is the place that you will tap or select.*

How to Customize Many Smart Stack Widgets On Homescreen

You customize many smart stack widgets on your home screen without taking many spaces or having them displaying separately on the screen. That is, you can have all selected smart stack widgets in a particular smart stack widget.

If you want to have many smart stack widgets in a smart stack, you have to ensure that you are selecting the same size of smart stacks of different features like weather, calendar, news, Siri suggestions, Photos... and more others.

Let us try the following features on your Homescreen:

1. Weather
2. Calendar
3. News
4. Photo
5. Reminder

You will need to follow the above steps of adding a widget on Homescreen to add each of the above-listed features. I will repeat the steps below for you to get used to it.

Note: I have already done Smart Stack Widget for Weather, you do not need to reselect weather again, continue from the next feature "Calendar"

Home Screen:

> ➢ On the Home screen press and hold till you will see a **sign of add** appear at the top left of the screen.
> ➢ Hit on the **Add sign.**

Widget Page:

> ➢ **Use Search Field:** Search for Calendar by typing the calendar into the **Search Field.**

- ➢ Hit on the Calendar keyword showing under the search field or tap on the **Search** button at the bottom right of the Keyboard.
- ➢ **Without Using Search Field:** once you open the Widget page, scroll down to select Calendar by tapping on it.
- ➢ Scroll to medium size of Smart Stack of Calendar.
- ➢ Hit on the **Add Widget** button at the bottom of the page.

Home Screen:

- ➢ The Calendar medium size of smart stack widget will appear below the Weather widget.
- ➢ **How to Merge Widgets:** Place your finger on it and move the Calendar widget on the Weather widget. Both will merge and become one smart stack widget.
- ➢ As you flip/scroll up or down of the smart stack widget you will see the Weather forecast for the day and Calendar.

Repeat the immediate above steps to select the widget for *News, Photo, & Reminder.*

How to Merge 2 or More Widgets Together

If you scroll up/down the widget, the weather widget will show

How to Customize Additional Small Widgets of Battery, & Clock

You can add small widgets of your own choice as you customized medium smart stack widgets above.

Home Screen:

➢ On the Home screen press and hold till you will see a **sign of add** appear at the top left of the screen.

➢ Hit on the **Add sign.**

Widget Page:

➢ **Use Search Field:** Search for **Battery** by typing battery into the **Search Field.**

➢ Hit on the Battery keyword showing under the search field or tap on the **Search** button at the bottom right of the Keyboard.

➢ **Without Using Search Field:** Once you open the Widget page, scroll down to select Battery by tapping on it.

➢ It will open the smallest widget page. If you scroll toward the left, the page will move to medium size page, then, scroll right to go back to the smallest page.

➢ Hit on the **Add Widget** button at the bottom of the page.

For Clock:

➢ Repeat the same steps for the Clock widget.

➢ When you get to the Widget page, scroll down to tap on the wall-clock image. Scroll from either right or left direction to see different types of a wall-clock.

➢ There are:
   • Small smart stack City Clock widget page

61

- Small smart stack World Clock widget page.
- Big smart stack World Clock widget page.

➢ Select either a small **Smart Stack Clock** or small **Smart Stack World Clock Widget**, so that you will be able to merge any of the selected small clock widgets with the previous small **Smart Stack Battery Widget** on your iPhone "If you want to".

➢ Hit on **Add Widget.**

➢ Hit on **Done** at the top right corner of the iPhone.

How to Merge Two or More Widgets on Homescreen and Search Page

If you are having two or more similar size of **smart stack widgets** on your iPhone and you want them to be viewed in a widget.

Take the following steps to combine the numerous widgets:

Home Screen or Search Page:

➢ Press and hold open space to unstable and make all the widgets and Apps shaking. (Don't let your finger press any app or widget because it will only highlight the app or widget you pressed).

Contained 5 Widgets

Widget

➢ Place your finger on each of them and be dragging them inside a particular widget at the top.

➢ By the side of the widget that contained other widgets, you will see vertical dots that show the number of widgets you have in it.

➢ Hit on **Done** at the top right corner of the screen.

➢ Scroll up or down of the Widget and see all the merged widgets.

Hint: All the combined widget will be automatically displaying one after the other at a particular time interval.

How to Completely Remove Customized Widgets

Home Screen or Search Page:

➢ Press and hold the Stack Widget till the Widget will come up with a Dialog Box containing the following options
  - Edit "Name of the Main Feature (e.g. Calendar)"
  - Edit Stack
  - Edit Home Screen
  - Remove Stack

➢ Tap on the **Remove Stack**
➢ A confirmation Dialog box will come up, hit on **Remove Stack** and immediately, the widget will disappear on the Home Screen or Searching Page.

Another Method of Removing Stack Widget

Home Screen or Search Page:

➢ Press and hold the open space of the Homescreen or Searching page till the minus sign "-" will show at the top left of the Widget and all Apps.
➢ Hit on the **Minus Sign** in a white circle. A dialog box will appear to activate your request.
➢ Hit on **Remove.**
➢ Go to the top right of the screen and tap on **Done.**

First Method To Remove Widget

Second Method To Remove Widget

How to Arrange Merged/Combined Widget

The arrangement is all about how you want all the combined widget to follow one another, that is, the first widget to be at the front, the second widget, the third widget... and so on.

63

These widgets will be automatically rotated as you arrange them by activating the **Rotate** switch.

The Step by Step Approach

Homescreen or Searching Page

> ➤ Press down the small **Smart Stack Widget** till you will see a **Dialog Box** come-up.
> ➤ **Dialog Box:** Select **Edit Stack**
> ➤ Hit on the **Smart Rotate Activator** to change from white to green .
> ➤ Press and drag any of the listed application stack widgets up or down to reach the position where you want it to be.
> ➤ When you are through then tap on close "x" at the top right corner of the page.

How to Edit Your Customized Widgets Stack

Homescreen or Searching Page

> ➤ Press and hold the **Smart Stack Widget** you want to **Edit.**
> ➤ A Dialog Box will come up, tap **Edit** the first option.
> ➤ An editing interface will come up. At the front of **Location** tap it and enter the name of the place. For instance,

> - **Clock**: You will enter the name of the City you want to check the time of the location.
> - **Weather**: You will enter the name of the location you want to see the present weather conditions and forecast.

Once you have entered the name of the location the clock will show you the exact time of the place; also for forecast, the details will be shown after you have entered the name of the location.

The Importance of Apps Library Page

This is another invention feature introduced in iOS 14 that you could use to search for App on your iPhone.

You could easily see this Apps Library page after you continuously swipe from the right side of the Home pages to the last Homescreen.

Apps are arranged in a box or group file according to their close relative functions. You can see a group of apps that you use regularly.

Also, there are groups of:

> ➢ Recently Added App
> ➢ Social Apps
> ➢ Productivity & Fitness Apps
> ➢ Utility Apps
> ➢ Creativity Apps
> ➢ Shopping & Food Apps
> ➢ Information & Reading Apps
> ➢ Suggestions Apps
> ➢ Entertainment Apps
> ➢ Travel Apps... and many others.

At the top of the page, you will see the Apps Library searching field that you can use to search any app.

In some **categories,** you will see a **sub-category** that shows 4 apps in the size of an App within the category.

You can select any of the App by tapping on each category as they are grouped on the screen.

You can still scroll down to search for different categories that are more relevant.

The App library will enable you to quickly know all the available apps that could be used for different helpful features with alternative apps in the same group.

How You Could Edit Plenty Homepages

This feature is a fantastic feature that will enable you to reduce the number of total homepages of your iPhone.

Presently you may have up to 6 and more homepages on iPhone due to several downloads of apps or customized widgets which are too much. You can reduce the number of homepages to fewer numbers of 2, 3, or 4.

Step by step of Editing your Homepage

Home Screen:

> ➤ Press and hold the open space of the screen for all the apps and widgets to be shaking and carry remove sign at the top left side.
> ➤ Tap on the **Pages Dots** below screen.

Edit Pages:

> ➤ All the total number of the pages will show on the **Edit Pages.**
> ➤ Hit the dot below each page image to check the number of Homepages you want to be

seeing on your iPhone.

➤ Hit on the **Done** option at the top right of the screen to return to the main Homepage.

➤ Swipe the screen from the right side of the screen to see all the checked/edited Homescreen. Look at the picture for a perfect guide.

Hint: You can repeat the above steps to either add or reduce Homepage(s) to the previous edited Homepages.

How You Could Rearrange App's Icons on the Homescreen

Apps could be moved from one place to another place on your iPhone Home screen. You may choose to rearrange the apps in alphabetical order or base on how you will be using them regularly or how they will be more convenient for you.

Homescreen: For a short time press hold the screen for an optional dialog box to appear.

Optional Dialog Box: Hit on the **Rearrange Apps** option. Immediate the entire apps will be shaking and unstable with the *Cancel sign* attached to the left top angle of each app.

Apps: Place your hand on each App you wanted to move and drag the app to the favorite place. As soon as, you are through with the rearranging of the Apps as you wanted then **Swipe Up** the screen from the bottom.

How You Can Keep Many Apps In A Customized File On Homescreen

Homescreen: For a short time press the screen for a dialog box to come up.

Dialog Box: Hit on the **Rearrange Apps** option. Immediate the entire apps will be stirring and unstable with the *Cancel sign* attached to the left top angle of each app.

Apps: Position your hand on an App and drag it to another app you want to keep in the same file. Before you release the dragged App on the below App make sure that a transparent white square shape appears around the below app. You will see the File Name text field above, hit on the text field to name the file.

If you want more than 2 Apps in a file, then continue dragging Apps on the file you have created and hit on the outer part of the file to restore and fix it.

As soon as, you are through with the rearrangement of the Apps as you wanted then **Swipe Up** the screen from the bottom, the whole apps will come back to normal.

How To Bring Out Those Apps From The Created Files

Created File

> ➤ **Two Apps in a File**, hold-down the file for a dialog box to show up for you to tap on **Rearrange Apps.** Immediately, the two Apps will be released from the file and show as an individual app on the Homescreen.
> ➤ **More than Two Apps in a File,** hold-down the file for a dialog box to show up, tap on **Rearrange Apps,** and all the Apps will be liberated.
> ➤ **If you want to be taken the Apps out of the file one after the other:**
>   > ✓ Hit the file the whole Apps will be seen boldly.
>   > ✓ Place your finger on any of the App and drag it out. The file will return to normal size while the

removed App will also appear normal on the Home screen.

➢ **Swipe up** from the bottom to stabilize the apps.

How You Can Delete Apps on the Homescreen

Homescreen

➢ Hold-down the app until you will see an optional dialog box.
➢ Hit on the **Delete** option. Immediately the app will be removed. *OR*
➢ Hold-down the app till you will see the whole app stirring and unstable with the Remove sign at the left angle of the apps.
➢ Hit on the **Remove sign**. Immediately the app will be removed from the page and the whole apps will automatically rearrange itself.
➢ **Swipe Up** to stabilize and normalize the apps.

How You Could Change Wallpaper of Lock Screen & Home Screen

Many lovely and attractive Wallpaper could be chosen to replace the default Wallpaper (a wallpaper that comes with the iPhone) through Settings. Apple had made a provision for many options for you to select. The Wallpaper is sectioned into four categories:

1. Dynamic Wallpaper
2. Still Wallpaper
3. Live Wallpaper
4. Photo Wallpaper

Dynamic Wallpaper: The wallpaper contains several circular bubbles in different sizes that slightly increase in size on the screen.

Still Wallpaper: The wallpapers have different attractive stable images and natural picture without movement.

Live Wallpaper: The wallpaper shows movement when you touch the screen. Any image that is chosen in this category for your either Lock screen or Homescreen moves when you press down the screen. You can preview the animation before you set it for either the Lock screen or Home screen.

Homescreen: Hit on the **Settings** icon.

Settings: Scroll down the page and select (hit/tap) **Wallpaper**

Wallpaper: Above the Lock Screen and Homescreen Image hit on **Choose A New Wallpaper.**

Choose: You will see Dynamic, Still, and Live galleries in a row with the series of your photo events arranged in the column below.

> ➢ Hit on any of the Wallpaper options provided or your customized personal photo.
> ➢ Hit on a Set option below the **Wallpaper**. But, if you do not like it, you may select **Cancel** to take you back to the Wallpaper Choose page to re-choose wallpaper.
> ➢ Optional Dialog Box will display three possible options that you may separately consider. There you can choose any of these options **Set Home Screen, Set Lock Screen,** or **Set Both.**
>
> **Set Home Screen:** The Wallpaper you have chosen will only appear on Home Screen.
>
> **Set Lock Screen:** The Wallpaper will only show on the Lock Screen.
>
> **Set Both:** The Wallpaper will show on both the Lock Screen and Home Screen. Therefore, you can choose two different Wallpaper for the two screens (i.e. Home & Lock Screens).

Homescreen Precautions

The Homescreen precautions will prevent your iPhone from performing any of these malfunctions like sudden sluggishness (moving slowly), jacking, delay or irregular response to finger touch, or auto-switch off.

1. Always ensure that all the open pages on your iPhone had been completely closed on your iPhone before you sleep the iPhone.
2. Ensure your iPhone is fully charged before you use it to browse, live chat, record longtime video or snap photo, download, upload… and many others.
3. Set *low power mode* on your iPhone to reduce the rate of energy consumption when battery capacity is 50 percent or less.
4. When the battery is low all the self-moving images (animation) like *Lock Screen Live Wallpaper* will stop working.

How to Move from Home Screen to Lock Screen

Homescreen to Lock Screen: Swipe down the left side of the Notch of your iPhone, alternatively place a finger at the bottom center of the Notch frame, and wipe down the screen toward the bottom of the iPhone. The Lock Screen will show.

How to Reduce Open Pages into the App icons on the Homescreen

Homescreen

> ➢ Hit on two-three different apps' icons on the Homescreen.
> ➢ Place your finger at the bottom center of the screen of the page.
> ➢ Slightly move up your finger for a small distance and take off your finger from the screen. You will see the app's page entering the app icon on the Homescreen.

How to See the Reduced or Minimized Apps' Pages

Homescreen (Middle Screen Expose)

> ➤ Move up your finger from the bottom center of the iPhone screen and slightly move it in an inverted seven ⌐ direction.
> ➤ As your finger is moving toward the right side of the iPhone you will see those open pages coming out from the left side of the screen.
> ➤ You can hit on any of the reduced opened app pages you still want to revisit to work on or get more information from.

Homescreen (Bottom Screen Expose)

> ➤ Place your finger on the first end of the horizontal Homescreen Bar at the bottom center of the iPhone and move your finger to the second end of the parallel bar.
> ➤ As you are moving the finger the page will be coming out one after the other. You can move from right to left or vice versa.
> ➤ Hit on any page you are looking for and it will fully display on the screen of the iPhone.

How to Completely Delete the Reduced Apps' Pages

Page Pressing Down Method (after the exposed steps)

> ➤ When you press down the minimized apps you have opened one by one for a while, they will show a **Remove Sign** (a red circle containing minus inside) at the left top edge of their pages. ⊖
> ➤ Hit the **Remove** sign to completely delete the minimized page(s).

Swiping Method (after the exposed steps)

> ➤ Place a finger on the individual reduced open app and swipe up further to completely remove the page from the iPhone.

The complete removal of the reduced opened pages on your iPhone regularly will prevent your iPhone from an abnormal slowdown of the iPhone speed efficiency

CHAPTER FOUR

How You Could Use Default & Customized Controls In Control Center of Your iPhone 12, Mini, Pro, or Max

Control Center is a slide page that contains all the basic application icons (symbols) that you can quickly get to on either iPhone Lock-Screen or Homescreen.

There are lots of apps with their operational icons on your iPhone Settings that can be customized to be in the Control Center for you to quickly reach.

Basically, by default the following apps and operational icons are in your Control Center:

- ✓ Airplane Mode
- ✓ Cellular Service
- ✓ Wi-Fi Network
- ✓ Bluetooth
- ✓ Music Panel
- ✓ Screen Lock Rotation Icon
- ✓ Do Not Disturb
- ✓ Screen Mirroring Icon
- ✓ Screen Light Control (Contains True Tone & Night Shift)
- ✓ Volume Control
- ✓ Flash
- ✓ Timer
- ✓ Calculator
- ✓ Camera

Airplane Mode Icon: It is used to keep your iPhone out of cellular service or network activity when you are on the Airplane board. It is activated when you hit on the icon surface.

Cellular Service Icon: It is used to activate the cellular service network provided by your SIM cellular provider. Hit on the surface of the icon to see the name of the network provider and active bar at the top right of your iPhone.

Wi-Fi Network Icon: This is a data-using network that could be activated through **Personal Hotspot** in the Settings or received from an external device like iPhone, Android, Mac, iPad, or PC hotspot via Wi-Fi connectivity.

Bluetooth Icon: This is used to receive or transfer any app data or document from, or to other Bluetooth supporting devices. Hit the surface of the icon to activate the features. You can use it to send sound from your iPhone to another **Bluetooth** supporting sound device to play the sound aloud. You can send one document at a time.

Music Panel: You can use this to play and regulate the sound volume of music from your *YouTube* or iPhone music sound. Hit on the surface of the *Play Panel* to control the sound.

Screen Lock Rotation: This will prevent your iPhone screen display to instantly move from portrait to landscape at any quick repositioning of the iPhone to  the landscape. Hit the icon to permanent the portrait screen display but if you want to use your iPhone to watch the **video** you can re-tap the icon to deactivate the effect.

Do Not Disturb: You can use it to stop your iPhone from ringing, vibrating, or notifying you when you are in an important gathering, meeting, on the Airplane board, or driving a car.

Screen Mirroring Icon: This will enable you to see what is on the screen of your iPhone on your Mac, PC, Projector, or TV through the use of a specific cable connector. Hit the surface of the icon to set the device connection and activate the application.

Screen Light Control: It is used to control the brightness and dimness of the screen light. If you want the screen light to be brighter, put your finger on the bright region of the control and move your finger up. But, if you want the screen face to look dim or dark move your finger from up to down.

When you press down the control **Night Shift** and   **True Tone** will appear below the screen.

You can further change the mode to **Night Shift** mode that will change the screen appearance to yellowish-cream like the evening period to protect your sight (eyes).

Although by default (i.e. from the factory) it is set to **True Tone**, the icon activation appears blue.

Volume Control: It is used to control ring tone, alarm, video, or audio sound volume on your iPhone. Place your finger on the surface of the volume icon and high the volume by moving up your finger or low the volume by moving down your finger.

Flash Icon: It is used to "On" **Touch/Flashlight** at the back of your iPhone. If you hit the **Flash icon** once immediately the Flashlight will display for you to see clearly or to make the back environment of your iPhone look like daylight and helps quick search.

Timer Icon: It is used to set various **Timer** formats and display the Timer on the **Homescreen.** Once you hit on the **Timer** icon you will access every detail of **Timer Setting.**

Calculator Icon: It is used for adding, dividing, subtracting, and multiplying numbers in mathematical calculations by mathematician, accountant, statistician, or everyone, and it can be extensively changed to a scientific calculator for a scientist to calculate advance calculation that involves cosine, sine, tangent, etc. Hit the **Calculator** icon for it to appear.

Camera Icon: It is quickly used to access a **Camera** page for you to take pictures and make videos. Tap on the Camera icon to get into the page instantly.

How You Can Add More of Apps' Controls in Control Center

Customize Apps into Control Center

Homescreen: Hit on **Settings Icon.**

Settings: Move down the page and hit on **Control Center**.

Control Center

> ➢ Hit on **Customize Control**.
> ➢ You will see **Access Within Apps**, put the activation button On if not activated by hitting on the activator.
> ➢ Hit on **Customize Control**.

Customize Control

> ➢ You will first see those controls that are in the Control Center listed above with a red circle having minus (remove) at the center that can be used to remove any of the controls from the Control Center if you deliberately hit on it.
> ➢ More listed Controls below are the available controls that you can add to those apps controls in the control center when you hit on the green circle having a cross sign (add) at the center. These are some of the controls you can add with those I have previously mentioned above:

Accessibility Shortcut, Apple TV Remote

Alarm, Magnifier, Text Size, Note, Guide Access, Do Not Disturb While Driving, Low Power Mode, Voice Mail, Stopwatch... and many others.

➢ Keep tapping on the **Back** icon at the top-left region of the iPhone to return to Homescreen or **Swipe Up** from the bottom center to return to Homescreen.

How You Could Create & Check Your Customized Controls in Control Center

View Controls on Lock Screen or Homescreen

➢ Place your finger at the top right side of your iPhone and swipe down

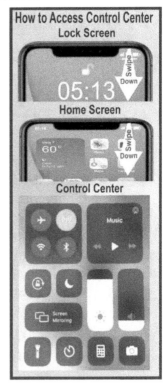

You will see the newly customized controls under the controls I have mentioned above.

If you do not see it, go back to Settings again to confirm if the control is still among the list of **Add More.** If you see it among the list, then hit on the **Add Circle** at the front of the control Icon to add it.

If it is not among **Add More** but among the list of those that are already in the control center then go back to the control center by swiping down the screen of the iPhone from the right side. Search carefully you will see it there.

How You Can Activate iPhone Screen Brightness from The Source

Homescreen: Hit on the **Settings Icon**.

Settings: Scroll down the page to hit on **Display & Brightness** to access the settings.

Settings: Hit on the **Brightness** activation slide to become green.

➤ Slide the Brightness adjuster from left to right to elevate/increase the screen light or slide the adjuster from left to right to reduce the screen light.

How Video and Music Can Be Taken from Other iPhones to Your iPhone 12, Mini, Pro, or Max

Settings on your iPhone and the other iPhone

Homescreen

➤ Go to **Control Center,** put On **Bluetooth,** and tap the screen, or swipe up from the bottom center to go back to the Homepage.

➤ Hit on **Settings**

Settings: Select (tap) on **General**

General: Hit on **AirDrop**

AirDrop: Select **Everyone** and swipe up to launch the Home screen or continually tapping on the **Back icon** at the top left of the screen till you get to the Home screen.

For iPhone Sending Video and Music (i.e. the iPhone Sending Video and Music)

Homescreen:

- ➢ **Videos**
    - ✓ Hit on **Photos Icon** to pick on a Video you want to select.

      Or
- ➢ **Music**
    - ✓ Hit on **Music Icon** and select your preferred music.
- ➢ Hit on **Share Icon**
- ➢ Select **AirDrop** by tapping on it.

On Your iPhone

- ➢ Tap on **Accept** in the optional notification of **AirDrop.**

On iPhone Sending Video and Music

- ➢ Hit on your iPhone Name you are sending items to.

Instantly the new iPhone would receive the selected item.

How You Can Use iTunes App on Your iPhone 12, Mini, Pro, or Max

The iTunes application is an important instrument as far as adding more bits of stuff to your iPhone through your PC by sending and getting more pictures, music, video, etc. on your iPhone.

Likewise, the iTunes Store could be used to download several videos or music and play them offline on your iPhone with the use of a Wi-Fi connection. Notwithstanding, the service does not go gratis (costless), that is, you will pay for every music or audio requested at the iTunes store.

Syncing your iPhone with iTunes to Get Additional Benefits

These are the following items you can add (sync) to iPhone from your iTunes library:

- ➢ Playlist,
- ➢ Movies
- ➢ Songs
- ➢ Podcasts
- ➢ Album
- ➢ Photo & Video
- ➢ Audiobooks
- ➢ Contact & Calendars

You should sync your iPhone with iTunes if you want to include the below items on your iPhone:

- ➢ **iTunes Playlists** but you will initially subscribe with **iTunes Match or Apple Music.**
- ➢ **Personal Video**
- ➢ **Calendars, Photos,** and **Contacts** provided you are not using **iCloud.**

You can also use iTunes to delete the formally added items from your iPhone.

All those lively benefits can be downloaded from the iTunes Store without you passing through the PC connection.

For you to get the iTunes Store App on your iPhone freely by using Password take the following step.

Homescreen

- ➢ Hit on **Settings Icon**

Settings: Hit on your Name or Sign In and select the **iTunes & App Store.**

iTunes & App Store: Hit on **Password Settings**

Password Settings

- ➢ Switch on Face ID for buying all you need.
- ➢ Below PURCHASE AND IN-APP PURCHASE hit on your desirable requirement (what you need).

- ➤ Below FREE DOWNLOAD you will see **Require Password**, hit the activator to become Green.
- ➤ As soon as, you are requested to provide your **Password,** then enter it.
- ➤ Hit on **OK.**

How You Send Audio Sound to AirPlay Speaker from Your iPhone 12, Mini, Pro, or Max

Homescreen: Go to **Control Center**

Control Center: Hit on the **Screen Mirroring** icon

Screen Mirroring: Press the **Audio Card** down for a few seconds and the **AirPlay** icon should be tapped on**.**

AirPlay Speaker: Hit the **AirPlay Speaker** to be connected.

Why You Need App Store on Your iPhone 12, Mini, Pro, or Max

With the use of the Apple Store App, you can completely download many apps like WhatsApp, Facebook, iMovie, Numbers, Keynote, Pages, GarageBand… and many others through the Apple store.

Homescreen: Hit on the **App Store** icon

App Store: Hit on the **Continue** bar.

Browsing Page: On a request dialog box showing on your screen, tap on **Don't Allow** for Apple store not to access your location.

App Search: Look down the lower left side of the screen to hit on **Search Icon.**

- ➤ Hit the search field to type in your app request.
- ➤ As soon as you seen the App below, hit on **"Get"** at the opposite for instant **Download**.
- ➤ Make Home **Swipe Up** to see the new App Icon.

How to Quickly Correct Malfunction or Stiffness Problem on Your iPhone

Unexpectedly, if your iPhone suddenly stops working or not responding to touch and the app(s) are not opening when you tap them then take the following steps to restart the iPhone.

Stop working at any page you are on your iPhone

Left Side of the iPhone

➢ Click **Up-Volume** button
➢ Click the **Down-Volume** button.

Right Side of the iPhone

➢ Use 11 seconds to press the **Power Switch** button.
➢ The iPhone will Switch Off and reboot itself to the Lock Screen.

Lock Screen

➢ Home Swipe Up (i.e. swipe up from the bottom center of the iPhone).
➢ Provide your **Passcode**
➢ Home Swipe Up.

How You Could Completely Setup Notification on Your iPhone

Homescreen: Hit on the **Settings** icon.

Settings: Move down and hit on **Notification**

Notification: Hit on the **App Store**

App Store: Give commands to your iPhone by activating the provided options that are including **Allow Notification, Badge App, Show on Lock Screen, Show in History, and Show as Banner.**

83

- ➢ Hit on any of these options below:
  - ✓ **Temporary Banner Show**
  - ✓ **Persistent Banner Show**
- ➢ Make Home **Swipe Up.**

For Your iPhone Notification Preview

It is optional for you to choose where you want the notification preview to be shown when the iPhone is locked or unlocked. After the above steps, hit on the **Back** icon for Notification at the top left of the screen to return to the **Notification Page.**

Notification: Select **Show Preview**

Show Preview: You may select **Always When Unlocked or Never.** But for privacy you may tap on **When Unlocked** that means, you can see the notification only when the iPhone is unlocked.

How To Salience Ringtone, Vibration, or Notification Alert

There are two major ways on your iPhone that you can use to prevent calls from ringing out or to avoid vibration or notification alert or alarm sound.

External Buttons

Silent Mode Button: This is the first small button on the left side of the iPhone that can be moved to the front and back direction of the iPhone.

When you move the small button from the front to the backside of the iPhone you will see red on the ground of the front space and at the top of the screen notification will be shown that **Silence Mode On**. This means that you have muted the iPhone, therefore, there will be no sound from a call, alarm, and notifications but it will vibrate if you have previously activated vibration during settings.

But, when you move the button from the back to the front of the iPhone the ringtone, alarm, and notification alert sound will restore (i.e. unmute).

Do Not Disturb

Lock Screen or Homescreen: Swipe down the screen from the top right side of your iPhone notch.

Do Not Disturb Icon: Hit on the **Do Not Disturb** feature to prevent ringtone and vibration from any call, message notification, alarm, and alert sound.

How To Make "Do Not Disturb" Work On Your iPhone

You will have to go to the Settings to make the feature of "Do Not Disturb" on your iPhone work by following these steps:

Homescreen: Hit on the **Settings** icon

Settings: Search down for **Do Not Disturb** and select it.

Do Not Disturb: Hit on the activation button to change to green.

How to Set a Schedule Time for Yourself

If you schedule the time you do not want people to disturb you with calls or messages then the first option of "Do Not Disturb" will be deactivated automatically because you cannot use both options at the same time. You have to choose either "Do not Disturb" or "Schedule".

Schedule: Hit on the Schedule, to set the time you don't want people to disturb you.

Specify Those Favorites That Your iPhone Can Allow

You have to choose some specific favorite contacts that must be excluded from **Do Not Disturb** settings. The **Favorite Contacts** maybe your Spouse, Children, Mother, Father, and Close Relatives that may seek your attention unexpectedly should in case of any unforeseen Emergency happen.

Allow Calls From: Hit on **Allow Call From** to select your favorites by tapping on the **Favorites** option.

Repeated Calls: Hit on the **Repeated Calls** Activation Switch to allow regular calls of your chosen favorites when you are busy till you pick it.

Activate: Hit on **Activate** to select **Manually** from the three available options which are:

1. Automatically
2. When Connected to Car Bluetooth
3. **Manually**

Manually you will always be able to activate **Do Not Disturb** through Control Center.

Auto-Reply To: Select **Auto-Reply** to choose the **Favorites** and **Auto-Reply Message** that will explain why you cannot pick-up your iPhone presently.

Wake & Sleep Actions

The feature will enable your iPhone to sleep and wake If you are working on your iPhone and you quickly want to arrive at the **Lock Screen** without you making regular backing of pages or swiping to Homescreen.

What you will do is to click the **Power/Switch Button** on the right side of the iPhone. Just a click the screen will go black meaning sleep and when you make a click again on the same **Power Button** the iPhone will awake at the **Lock Screen.**

Meanwhile, any of the security authentications like Face ID or Passcode may probably require. If your Face ID failed your Passcode will be automatically displayed for you to enter.

Auto-Sleep

Your iPhone may sleep automatically if the idle time (the time you are doing anything) has passed the time frame you set in the Settings for the iPhone screen activities, therefore, your iPhone will sleep. Wake the screen by clicking the **Switch Button** to wake it on the same page you have stopped working.

How to Preserve Cellular Data on Your iPhone

The use of this feature will perfectly save your cellular data from those apps that use cellular data to carry out an automatic update on your iPhone.

Homescreen: Hit on the **Settings**

Settings: Select **Cellular**

Cellular: Opposite **Cellular Data** hit on **Roaming Off.**

Turn On the activation switch of **Low Data Mode** to green.

How You Can Ensure Low Power Mode Battery Manager

The low battery mode will increase the strength of your iPhone battery energy when the battery has discharged up to half of the stored power of the battery.

However, when you have set the battery mode on your iPhone to be active at a 50% charged level of the battery; it will actively reduce many apps that are more using energy of the battery on your iPhone.

As a result, the brightness of the screen light will be regulated according to the level of brightness you have set for **Low Power Mode** in the settings.

The Live Wallpaper will stop working when battery mode is active.

Activate Through Settings

Homescreen: Hit on the **Settings Icon.**

Settings: Move down the page to hit on **Battery**

Battery:

> ➢ Hit on the **Low Power Mode** to be activated by changing the button to Green.
> ➢ Go back to the Home screen by backing the pages or swiping up from the bottom center of the iPhone.

Activate Through Control Center

You can quickly activate the **Low Power Mode** Manually if you have customized the control through settings. If you want to know how to customize control, go to Guide Three and read how to **add more of the apps' controls in the Control center**.

Homescreen/Lock Screen: Place your hand at the right side of the Notch above and swipe down to launch **Control Center.**

Control Center: Hit on **Low Power Mode** icon to activate the feature on the iPhone. The icon surrounding will change to white and the battery charge level will be yellow if it is activated.

How You Can Improve Battery Life-Time Through Auto-Lock Control

Auto-lock comes to action immediately after the idle time interval you have set has elapsed. That is, the iPhone will automatically lock itself after the seconds or minutes you have given to your iPhone to be active when you have stopped using it has passed.

In the Settings, you can instruct your iPhone to lock itself at any of this period below or you may even choose "Never" which is not helpful to the iPhone Battery.

➤ 30 Seconds
➤ 1–5 Minutes

Homescreen: Hit on **Settings Icon.**

Settings: Gently move down the page to select **Display & Brightness.**

Display & Brightness

➤ Hit on the **Brightness** activating switch to become Green.
➤ As you have activated the switch the Brightness regulator will be active. Then Move the Brightness regulator toward the left to reduce the light intensity.

Night Shift: If you have not activated the **Night Shift** hit on it and put it "ON". After you have activated it, go to the Control center to deactivate it by pressing down the **Screen Light Control** (Brightness control) and hit on **True Tone.**

Auto-Lock: Hit on the Auto-Lock to select your preferred time that you want your iPhone to remain active when you are doing anything.

Rise to Wake: Put "On" the activator, so that you may hit your iPhone screen when it is about to sleep.

Text Size: If you are not satisfied with the font size of the whole text on your iPhone you can go ahead and hit the **Text Size.** Move the Knob regulator toward the right to enlarge the text size on your iPhone screen. But, If, it is already too large, you can then move the knob regulator toward the left. (Optional)

Bold Text: You can make all the text on your iPhone screen to appear bold if you are not satisfied with the current look of the text font on your iPhone.

Hint: If you alter the text size or bold text, it will surely affect all the words on your iPhone.

How You Can Instantly Make Emergency Free Call on Your iPhone

You have to know the quick ways of activating emergency calls and the quick approach of making the call when you noticed or experienced danger around you that may result in loss of treasure or life if you do not get expert attention urgently.

Switch Button: Click the **Switch Button** 5 times.

Homescreen: Hit on the **Settings Icon.**

Settings: Move down to hit on **Emergency SOS**

Emergency SOS: Hit on **Also Works with 5 Clicks.**

Anytime you noticed a sudden attack or unforeseen danger, all you need to do is to click the Switch Button 5 times, and instantly you will be connected to **Emergency SOS.**

Other Method

Press down **Switch Button** and **Up Volume** together for the **Emergency SOS** screen to show up.

At the center of the screen, you will see **SOS Switch.** Slide the **SOS** Switch from left to right side to be connected to Emergency Call.

Hint: You can also switch off your iPhone on the same page by moving **Power Switch** from left to right.

CHAPTER FIVE

How To Completely Use New Translate App and Siri Translation

How You Can Use Translate App To Translate English in Ten Languages on Your iPhone

 Translate App is newly introduced in iOS 14 to *translate English (UK), English (US), Arabic, Mandarin Chinese, French, German, Italian, Japanese, Korean, Portuguese, Russian, and Spanish* languages without connecting your iPhone to the network (No Cellular Network and Wi-Fi Network). It can be used offline.

You can use it to translate your text before you send it on your iMessage chat. It is an amazing platform for chatting with a different individual speaking different languages.

You don't have to be worried about having a French-speaking person as your best friend. More so, you could use it to relate with other business partners speaking any of the 12 supported languages.

You can use it to translate foreign languages into your speaking and comprehensive language.

The easiest method of using it is by using the Audio Speech recording that will convert all your words into text messages on the screen.

You can also enter text directly on the screen and once you have completed the text tap on the other language you have selected e.g. French.

Step by Step for Translate App

After setup, the Translate App is supposed to be among the Homepage Apps but do not see it on time, or you want to be very sure and fast about the searching do any of the two options under **Homescreen** below.

How to locate the Translate App

Homescreen:

> ➤ **Method 1**: Slight swipe down the top center of the screen for Search Bar to show.
> ➤ **Method 2**: Gently look through the Apps on the Homepages.
> ➤ **Method 3**: Alternatively, swipe left to Apps Library to search for **Translate App**.
> ➤ Tap the **Translate App** to open the app page.

Translate App:

> ➤ There are two language selecting buttons at the top of the page each of them has the first common language English (US) / (UK).
> ➤ If you are a United Kingdom or United State English Speaker, hit on the left side button and select either English (UK) or English (US).
> ➤ Tap on the top right language selecting the button to check the language you want your text messages or speech to be translated to. You can choose from the supported languages e.g. German.
> ➤ **For the Audio Speech Translation only**. Position the iPhone screen to be in the landscape by going to the

Control Center and tap on **Screen Rotate Icon.**

How to Get the Translate App on Homescreen
Method 1: Swipe Down & Search
Method 2: Look Through Apps
Method 3: Search Through App Library

Text Translation

- Hit on the surface of **"Enter Text",** a keyboard will appear.
- On Portrait (Normal) Screen: As you are entering your text, immediately the translation will be appearing under.

Speech Translation

- On Portrait Screen: You can alternatively use the audible speech option by tapping on the Microphone icon  at the bottom center of the screen
- On Landscape Screen: Hit on the **Microphone Icon** at the bottom center of the page.
- Immediate the Sound Wave will appear as you are saying the words of the language you have selected; they will be converted to text.
- As soon as you have stopped your speech, it will take a few seconds for the text to be translated to the other selected language.
- You can listen to the translation by tapping the

Play Button  at the bottom right of the screen. It will automatically stop as soon as it is finished. But, if you do not want it to finish, then you can hit on the same button.

- Save the translated text into Favorites for the future purpose by tapping on a **Star** icon at the immediate bottom left of the translated text.

Why Need to Save Your Translated Speech in the Favorites

Your translated speech could be reused anytime when it is saved as the **Favorite**.

The Step by Step

> ➤ When you open the **Translate app**, you will see the **Favorites icon** at the bottom right of the page.

> ➤ Hit on the **Favorite Icon** . The list of the recent translated speech will show first and by the other translated speeches arrange according to the period you have taken them.

> ➤ Scroll search the page to locate the **Translated Speech**.

> ➤ Hit on the **Translated Speech** you want to use.

How to Expand the Translated Language and Cover the Whole Screen

If previously in Portrait position

> ➤ Enable **Rotate Icon** at the Control Center.
> ➤ Turn the iPhone to be in a Landscape position.
> ➤ Hit on **Expand Icon** at the bottom left of the screen to fully cover the whole screen with an attention green background effect.

Hint: For you to minimize the translated text hit on the **Minimize**

Icon at the bottom left.

Importance of Favorites

How to Use Translate App without Network

For you to access the offline Apple translate app, then you will need to use a Wi-Fi network to download the language packages in order to create iPhone build-in translation.

The Step by Step:

> ➤ For you to have the package, select the exact language for example France
> ➤ Scroll down to **"Available Offline Languages"**.
> ➤ Locate the language you want to download and hit on the upside-down arrow in a circle to enable **Download.** ⊕
> ➤ **To Delete the Package**: Swipe left the downloaded package and select the **Delete** option.

How to translate One-on-One discussion

The Step by Step:

Homepage: Hit on the **Translate App to** launch the page

Translate Page: Hit on the **top language buttons**.

➤ Scroll down to activate the **Automatic Detection** switch to recognize the communicator language.
➤ Hit on the Microphone Icon and speak as soon as you are set. Immediately, the Translate app will recognize the language then ask the second person to tap the Microphone again and speak.
The translator will translate the spoken words into the English language.

All the conversations that both of you have said so far will the displayed on the translation platform by scrolling down the page.

How You Could Edit Wrong Interpretation Correctly

In any occasional situation whereby you noticed your speech is been wrongly translated.

All you need to do is to hit on the speech transcript and correctly edit the mistake. It is as simple as that.

Then you can replay the speech transcript for the partner to read.

How You Could Use Siri To Translate English Text To Ten Different Languages

This is an amazing new development in the use of the Siri App on the latest iPhone 12, Mini, Pro, and Max.

In iOS 14 Siri could go as far as translating English text into ten different supported languages that include Arabic, German, Spanish, French, Italian, Japanese, Brazilian Portuguese, Russian, and Mandarin Chinese respectively.

Therefore, it will be advisable for you to first and foremost understand the different languages that are supported by Siri.

If you are not sure that the second language is supported by Siri then you may ask Siri to tell you the supported languages.

Step by Step of What to Do

First Method

- Press the Siri Button and say:
- Hey Siri! what languages can you translate into English?
- Immediately, Siri will list all the supported languages.
- Siri will say; Ok, What would like to translate?
- Then tell Siri what you want to translate, immediately, Siri will generate the translation in the language you have chosen.

Second Method

- Press the Siri Button
- Say, Hey Siri, Can you translate English text to German?
- Siri will say; Sure, what would like to translate.
- Then tell Siri what you want to translate into German. (e.g. Hey Siri1 What is "*How are do I celebrate the end of the year party*" in the German language.).

How to Use Make-Up Recognition to Draw Perfect Shapes On Note, Mail, Photo, Messages, Files, and Safari

The new advanced in-built shape recognition in the latest iOS 14 running in iPhone 12, Mini, Pro, and Max will perfectly enable every individual to achieve correct shapes of different structures.

You do not need to look for a ruler or searching for any shape that is very close to your dream shape. Now the new iOS 14 has a diverse shape recognition that can perfectly actualize your main dream through your rough hand shape sketch.

Generally, the automatic shape recognition has been built-in the **Make-Up Tool** in all apps that make use of drawing shapes which include **Photo, Note, Book, Mail, Files, Messages,** and **Safari.**

These are the different shapes you can draw:

- ✓ Lines
- ✓ Arrow Head with Line
- ✓ Outline Arrow
- ✓ Squares
- ✓ Rectangles
- ✓ Triangle
- ✓ Right or Left Angle
- ✓ Equilateral
- ✓ Isosceles
- ✓ Circle
- ✓ Speech Bubbles
- ✓ Arcs
- ✓ Arrow Heads with Arc
- ✓ Pentagons
- ✓ Ellipses
- ✓ 90° Curve Line
- ✓ Clouds
- ✓ Stars
- ✓ Outline Stars
- ✓ Crisscrossed Line
- ✓ Hearts

Step by Step for Note App:

Homescreen: Hit on **Note app**,

Note Page: If you are having text to write before the shape do the following step first.

> - Hit on the screen for the Keyboard to show up. Tap on the **Pencil Icon**..
> - Alternatively, go to the bottom left of the screen, select **Pencil** in the **Shape Tool**
> - Use your finger to draw a shape that will join with the

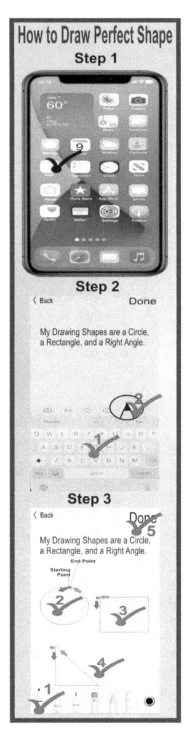

98

starting point of the shape and wait for a few seconds for it to be transformed into a perfect shape before you remove your finger.

➢ As soon as you are satisfied with the shape you hit on **Done** at the top right corner of the page.

CHAPTER SIX

Fantastic Ways Use Camera and Photo Apps on Your iPhone Professionally

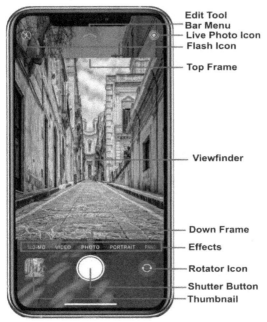

You can use the Camera app to access saved photos through Thumbnails and take pictures of every image around you. The Camera is designed to take a live picture and modified compressed Panorama images. All the captured photographs are automatically saved in Photo Library.

In the Camera interface, you will see options that can be used to take different pictures and what you can do to add more attraction to the pictures.

The Camera can be used to take photographs of anything including flowering plants, animals, human and nonliving things at the back and front of your iPhone by tapping on the Camera rotating icon which "I called Camera Rotator" that can change the back facing Camera to front-facing Camera to take Selfie.

The different modes in your Camera are including Video, Time-Lapse, Slo-Mo, Pano (Panorama), Portrait, and Photo Mode.

When your iPhone iOS 13 is upgraded to iOS 13.2 and above you will see a more beneficial feature like Deep Fusion.

To add more lovely effects to your picture, you can use Filter, Night Mode, Live Photo, and Burst.

What You Can See On the Camera Screen

1. Flash Icon: It is at the top left angle of the screen.
2. Night Mode Icon: It is located by the immediate side of the Flash.
3. Live Photo Icon: It is located at the top right angle of the screen.
4. Edit Toolbar Menu Icon: It is located at the top center of the screen.
5. View Frame: It is located at the center of the screen where the image will appear.
6. Zoom Range: It is at the base of the View Frame to adjust the size of your image.
7. Camera Modes in Row: It is at the top of the Shutter frame.
8. Thumbnail: It is at the left bottom of the screen to show a newly snapped image.
9. Shutter Button: It is at the bottom center of the screen to snap image(s).
10. Camera Rotator Icon: It is at the bottom right of the screen.

The various ways through which you can access Camera on your iPhone:

Lock-Screen

➢ Slide your iPhone screen from the right side to the left at the Lock-screen.
➢ Hit on the **Camera icon** at the bottom right of the iPhone screen.

Homescreen

➢ Hit on the **Camera Icon**
➢ Position the Camera to pace the image at the center of the View Screen.

101

➤ Hit on the **Shutter** or Up or Down Volume Button on the left side of your iPhone.

For You To Secure Your Photograph

Homescreen: Hit on **Setting Icon**

Settings: Select **Camera**

Camera: Select **Preserve Settings**

Preserve Settings: Put On the **Live Photo, Camera Mode,** and **Creative Control** Activators.

The Effects & Importance of Rear Camera
1. *Wide Angle Camera of 12MP f/1.6.*
2. *Ultra-Wide Camera of 12 MP/2.4*
3. *Telephoto Camera of 12 MP f/2.0.*

1. *Telephoto Camera* will enable you to optically zoom in image two times (4x) when you tap on the 1x zoom icon at the bottom of the Viewfinder without losing the original quality of the image.
*Hint: If you have your view in one time (1x) zoom you are using a normal standard camera which is called a **Primary Camera,** but if you zoom in the image 4x you have a chance to a Telephoto camera which is the **Secondary Camera.***

2. *Telephoto Camera* will also enable you to effectively use Portrait light effect options on your Photograph. When you swipe the Viewfinder from right to left (left swipe/swipe over) to select **Portrait view**.
The portrait will let you select the focus point of the image by tapping the major part of the image for your camera to focus.
When you make the focus point a white square will appear to surround the target part of the image.

The surrounding light of the focused object will gain different background colors which are known as **Focus Effect.**

Hint: When you hit on a box frame containing a ball inside for **Normal** light of Portrait lighting mode in an anticlockwise direction to select other light modes, the camera will switch to the Telephoto Camera to add different light effects (focus effects) around the image.

The Portrait Lighting Mode is including Video, Time-Lapse, Slo-Mo, Pano (Panorama), Portrait, and Photo Mode

How To Achieve Sharp Photo & Distinct Background in the Dark Surrounding

To overcome poor light or dark surroundings, Apple introduces a sophisticated *Light Detection and Ranging (LiDAR)* Scanner for Night Mode Portrait.

It has rapid autofocus in poor light to produce distinct background and cop-out the real images, and carry-out next stage of Augmented Reality (AR).

It could be used to rearrange the position of the images on your portrait coverage.

When you press and hold any farther image, move it close to the other image(s) to remove in-between distance.

To prevent night defects on your photograph you have to make use of **Night Mode** Features that will completely remove shadow or reflection of darkness on your picture outcome.

Look at the top left side of the Camera interface you will see Flash and Night mode, when you tap on Flash automatically Night Mode will OFF but when you tap on Night Mode instantly Flash will go OFF.

When you hit on the **Night Mode** again it will disable the feature: More so, your iPhone will automatically show Night Mode to control the light around the image when the surrounding is dark.

How You Can Take Portrait Photo

You can take photos in a portrait by positioning your iPhone in the normal vertical position █ or landscape ▄▄ by making the iPhone to be positioned in a horizontal position (i.e. move the iPhone long side in 45° to ground level).

Homescreen: Hit on **Camera Icon**

Camera

> ➢ Hit on **PHOTO**
> ➢ Position the Camera either in Portrait or in Landscape.
> ➢ Let the image be at the center of Camera View.
> ➢ Hit the **Shutter** or click any of the Volume buttons at the side of your iPhone.
> ➢ You will see the photo in the **Thumbnail** below.
> ➢ Hit on the **Thumbnail** to review the Photo.
> ➢ You may also go to the Photo app to select your snapped picture.
> ➢ **To Delete:** Hit on Photo App and hit on all the pictures you want to delete and hit on **Waste Bin** at the bottom right of the screen.

Portrait Photo

It is an amazing invention of Photo modification the can make your Photo come out in various professional light to enhance the quality of the image.

The loaded lights are Natural, Studio, Contour, Stage, Stage Light Mono, and High-Key Light Mono respectively.

Camera Interface

➤ Look at the lower base of the View Frame scroll from either left to right or right to left to hit on **PORTRAIT.**

➤ Once you position your iPhone in Portrait the various light will show above the lower region of the View frame in arc direction.

➤ Hit the ball one by one to see its light effect on the image. Scroll toward the left to see the rest of the light.

➤ Let your image be either automatic focus (rectangular) at the center of the Viewfinder or hit any location on the screen to make your focus point.

➤ Hit on Shutter to snap the image. You can also do the same for yourself.

Pano Mode (Panorama)

Homescreen: Hit on **Camera Icon**

Camera Interface

➤ Look at the lower base of the View Frame scroll from either left to right or right to left to hit on **Pano.**

➤ First, let the Camera capture the left end of the image.

➤ View it in the rectangle Image View

➤ Hit on Shutter to start capture

➤ Slowly move your hand straight from the left edge side of the Image to the right edge side of the image. Use the Arrow on a straight line to guide your straight movement.

➤ Hit on the same Shutter to stop the shot.

➤ The Image will be spherically wide in size and look beautiful.

➤ You can also use it to make Selfies in the same method.

Live Photo

Homescreen: Hit on **Camera Icon**

- Look at the lower base of the View Frame scroll from either left to right or right to left to select **Photo**
- Hit on the **Live** icon at the top right side of the Camera interface, the icon will change to yellow and you will see LIVE at the top center of the page.
- Let the Camera capture image correctly within a rectangle that is automatically showing at the center of the view fame.
- Hit on Shutter to take a shot of the image.
- The Image will be saved in the Photo library as Live Photo.

Zoom Capture

The Zoom sizes are shown at the lower base of the View Frame. If the image you want to capture is very small in the **Camera View** you can hit on either time 1 or times 2 to enlarge the image on your screen.

Finger Method

You can place your thumb and a finger on the screen and move them away from each other to enlarge the image or pitching the screen to reduce the image. When you move the two fingers together it will reduce the image size.

Zoom Magnification:

- The iPhone 12 & Mini have optical zoom out of times two and times three of digital zoom up.
- The iPhone 12 Pro has optical zoom out & in of times two and times six of digital zoom up.
- The iPhone 12 Pro Max has optical zoom out of time two and a half, and zoon in times two with times seven digital zoom up.

Add Effect on a Saved Photo in the Library

- ➤ Camera Interface: Look at the bottom left of the Camera you will see a small rectangle show image, it is called **Thumbnail**.
- ➤ It the **Thumbnail** to view the recent image on the screen. Swipe from right to left to see more pictures you have shot before.
- ➤ Stop at the image you want to edit.
- ➤ Look at the top center you will see a menu minimized arrowhead which is called **Edit Menu** .
- ➤ Hit on the **Menu Toolbar** for a dropdown of different Edit options will appear.
- ➤ Select **Filter** and you will see the chosen image appear in different thumbnails with different color effects on each image replicate.
- ➤ Select the one like.
- ➤ Hit on **Done** to save the selected image.

Add Effect on the Captured Image

- ➤ Camera Interface: Look at the top center you will see a menu minimized arrowhead which is called **Edit Menu.**
- ➤ Hit on the **Menu Toolbar** for a dropdown of different Edit options will appear.
- ➤ Select **Filter** and you will see different thumbnails with different color attractions.
- ➤ Scroll from right to left and select any of the thumbnails with lovely color influence. The color will transform the image and the environment look.
- ➤ Hit on Shutter to take your shot.
- ➤ The newly captured image will be seen in the bottom left **Thumbnail**.

Use Burst Shot for Multiple Photo Shots at a Goal

It will enable you to take a continuous photo shot that you can later select the nice pictures among the total shots.

➢ **Camera Interface**: Let your iPhone Camera be positioned at the image.
➢ Use your finger to move the **Shutter** to the left without you lifting your finger till you complete all the number of **Burst Shots** you wanted to take at a time.
➢ The Camera will continually snap the image.
➢ Remove your finger from the Shutter, for it to return to the center and stop the continuous shots.

How to Quickly Capture Video from Photo Mode without Selecting Video Mode

You can quickly take video recordings when you are in Photo mode taking photos.

All you need to do is to press down the **Up Volume Button** to open the Video Mode and start recording.

Once you release your thumb, immediately the video recording will stop.

How To Get Perfect Video Recording & Watching

On this latest iPhone 12, Mini, Pro, and Max you can achieve perfect Video watching on YouTube App with the highest 4K at 60fps HDR by performing the setting through the YouTube screen.

Homescreen: Open the YouTube App.

YouTube Page:

➢ Select the **Video** you want to watch through the Search bar.
➢ On the "Video screen" look at the top left of the screen to tap on **Ellipsis Icon** ⦂ for the menu. The following menu will show:
  • **Quality**
  • Captions
  • Report
  • Help & Feedback
  • Playback speed
  • Cancel

- ➢ Select **Quality** and you will see the following HDR qualities:
  - • Auto (720p60 HDR)
  - • **2160p60 HDR**
  - • 1440p60 HDR
  - • 720p60 HDR
  - • 480p60 HDR
  - • 360p60 HDR
  - • 240p60 HDR
  - • 144p60 HDR
- ➢ Select the highest HDR which is **2160p60 HDR** of 4K.
- ➢ You can play the video to watch it at the best resolution.

How You can Select the Highest Resolution through Settings

The Video mode is similar to Slo-Mo processes. The output of the Video will be accurate with the original movement without any delay.

To have the best of the Normal Video and Slo-Mo Video production on your iPhone with the highest quality resolution you have to initially do the following regulation in the Settings before you start the recording.

Homescreen: Hit on **Settings Icon**

Settings: Select **Camera**

Camera: Hit on **Record SLO-MO**

> **Record SLO-MO:** Select **1080p HD** at **240fps** (frame per second), return to **Camera** settings by hitting on **Back Icon** at the top left of the screen

Camera: Hit on **Record Video**

Record Video

- ➢ Select **4k at 60fps**.
- ➢ Hit on **Back Icon** to return to **Camera** settings.

109

Camera: Hit on **Format**

> Format: Hit on **High Efficiency**

➢ Return to the **Homescreen.**

Homescreen: Hit on **Camera App Icon**

Camera Interface

➢ Select **Video** from the Camera Modes below the View margin.
➢ Hit on the Red Recording Button to **Start** the recording.
➢ Hit on the button again to Stop the **Video Recording.**

Slo-Mo (Slow Motion)

You can apply motion with a timer to beautify modeling, sports activities, production stages, advertisement, growth... and many others.

Camera Interface: Below the View-frame scroll the Camera mode and hit on **Slo-Mo**.

➢ Position your iPhone either in Portrait or Landscape the best way you want it.
➢ Hit on the Red Recording Button at the bottom center to start your either **Selfie Slo-Mo** or Scene/Event/Action taking place at the front of your Camera.
➢ Hit on the Red Recording Button again to Stop the **Slo-Mo Recording.**
➢ **To Play Your Recorded Slo-Mo:** Go to Homescreen and hit on **Photo App.**
➢ Hit on the **Slo-Mo** and it will play. You can share with your friends in iMessage, Social Media by tapping **Share Icon** at the bottom of the screen.

How You Could Use Pano Mode (Panorama)

Homescreen: Hit on **Camera Icon**

Camera Interface

- ➢ Look at the lower base of the Viewfinder Frame scroll from either left to right or right to left to hit on **Pano.**
- ➢ First, let the Camera capture the left end of the image.
- ➢ View it in the rectangle Image View
- ➢ Hit on Shutter to start capture
- ➢ Slowly move your hand straight from the left edge side of the Image to the right edge side of the image. Use the Arrow on a straight line to guide your straight movement.
- ➢ Hit on the same Shutter to stop the shot.
- ➢ The Image will be spherically wide in size and look beautiful.
- ➢ You can also use it to make Selfies in the same method.

How to remove vertical & horizontal lines on your Camera screen

The line is very useful for you to properly position your image at the center of the Camera's Viewfinder. But if you do not need it, then go to:

Homescreen: Hit on the **Settings** icon.

Settings: Select **Camera**

Camera

- ➢ Hit on the **Grid** activation switch to deactivate it. The switch will change from green to white as it was shown above.
- ➢ Swipe Up to go back Home.

Homescreen: Hit on the **Camera icon**

Camera: On the Camera's Viewfinder you will not see the lines (Grid) again. But if you later want the line to reappear on the screen, then go back to the above steps of deactivation to hit on the

Grid activation switch to change from white to green.

Hint: If you snapped an image when the grid is on the screen, the lines will not appear on the snapped picture. It is used as a guide.

How to Use Your iPhone Camera to Scan Quick Response (QR) Code

Quick Response (QR) Code activation will enable your camera to scan QR code that will allow you to go to a website without you typing the *web address* on your iPhone browser **web tab** of Safari.

First and foremost you have to activate the function in the Camera Settings to enable the QR Code recognizing feature.

How to Activate the Camera QR Code Scanner

Homescreen: Hit on the **Settings** icon.

Settings: Select **Camera**

Camera

> ➢ Hit on the **Scan QR Code** activation switch to activate it.
> ◗◯. The switch will change from white to green.
> ➢ Swipe Up to go back to Homescreen.

How you can use the Camera App to Scan the QR Code on your iPhone

Lock Screen or Homescreen or Control Center: Hit on the **Camera icon**

Camera

> ➢ Ensure that you are using the Rear (Back) Camera. If not, hit on the **Camera** turning icon (rotator) 🔄 at the bottom right of the screen to turn the camera view to the rear Camera.
> ➢ Position your camera to focus on the Quick Response Code.
> ➢ A notification will show up on your screen for you to open the **Website** link (e.g. Open "amazon.com" in Safari).

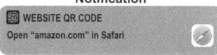

Notification

WEBSITE QR CODE
Open "amazon.com" in Safari

➢ Hit on the notification to open the website link with the **Quick Response**.

How to Use High Dynamic Range (HDR) Camera to Produce Outstanding Photo Shoots

The use of High Dynamic Range (HDR) will make your pictures look more colorful, real, and attractive.

It could enable **Automatically** or **Manually.** When the camera is set to Auto HDR every Photoshoot that will be taken will be automatically beautified with perfect color and awesome effect.

But if you disable Auto HDR, you will see the option of HDR at top of the Viewfind for you to tap and select from the menu including **Auto, On,** and **Off**.

If you select the **On** option before you take any picture, you have to enable the manual function of the HDR effect on the picture.
HDR

When you select the **Off** option from the menu then you have disabled the function of HDR on every picture that you will be taken after. **HDR**

But, if you select the **Auto** option that means you have manually chosen Auto HDR which could be also off by tapping on the HDR menu at the top of the Viewfinder.

However, if you prefer having the HDR option to be permanently fixed to Auto HDR without showing the icon at the top menu, then you have to Settings to get it done.

Homescreen: Hit on the **Settings** icon

Settings: Select **Camera**

Camera

> Hit on the **Auto HDR** activation switch to change to green.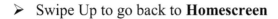

> Swipe Up to go back to **Homescreen**

Homescreen: Launch your **Camera** by tapping on the Camera icon.

Start taking your pictures. All your pictures will be automatically enhanced with high dynamic range color effects and come out pretty good.

How To Backup All The Saved Pictures With iCloud Photo Library

This will quickly save all your photos and video iCloud storage to prevent total loss when your iPhone is lost or suddenly develops a technical problem that may cause your iPhone to delete all the documents on it. But, since they have been saved in the iCloud Photo Library, you could recover all back on your iPhone completely.

Homescreen: Hit on the **Settings** icon

Settings: Select **Photo**

Photo: Hit on **iCloud Photo Library** activation switch to change to green, .

Swipe up from the bottom center to return to **Homescreen.**

Homescreen: Press the Siri button and ask Siri:

Hey Siri! Show me all Photos that were taken yesterday

Immediately, all the pictures you took yesterday will display for you to see on your screen.

114

How to permit Siri to search Photos on your iPhone

When you enable Siri to always search for any particular photo for you on the iPhone, it will quickly provide all the requested Photos within a second.

Homescreen: Hit on the **Settings** icon

Settings: Select **Photo**

Photo

- ➢ Hit on **Siri & Search**
- ➢ Hit on **Search & Siri Suggestions** activation switch to change to green,

On the same page of PHOTO you can activate the following options to improve easy accessibility:

1. **iCloud Photo Sharing** : This will create albums to share with other people, or subscribe to other people's shared albums.

2. **Summarize Photos** : The Photos tab will show every photo in your library in all views. You can choose compact, summarized views for Collection and Year.

3. **View Full HDR** : It will automatically adjust the display to show the complete dynamic range of Photos.

4. **Show Holiday Events** : **Under Memory,** this will enable you to see holiday event for your Home Country.

5. **Automatic:** Under Transfer to MAC or PC, you can tap this option also to be checked in order to automatically transfer Photos and Video in a compatible format, or always transfer the original file without checking for compatibility.

6. Select **Keep Original.**

Hint: Do not enable Cellular Data to download Photos or Videos, therefore, deactivate the activation switch of **Cellular Data** when you tap on it. This will save your cellular data from being used up quickly.

Always use a Wi-Fi network connection to download photos and videos by going to Control Center and select Wi-Fi Icon.

How You Can Use Professional Camera App To Boost Your Photograph Quality

 If you want to be using your iPhone professional photography then you will need to know to control the Picture(s) Manual Shutter Speed, ISO, Exposure... and many others, for you to get an amazing outstanding picture(s)

Therefore, you will download an additional Camera App called **ProCamera** that will enable you to have access to a menu that contains many editing tools you could use to improve the general quality of the Photo.

When you launch the ProCamera App, it will show the normal Camera App look with an advanced feature of exposure control under Viewfinder for you to regulate the picture exposure to be brighter or darker when you place your finger on the **Zero (O)** Calibrated Pointer and slide the control pointer toward the right to increase the exposure brightness or toward the left to increase the exposure darkness.

How to Access Professional Menu

After you have downloaded ProCamera on your iPhone:

Homescreen: Hit on ProCamera App.

On the Camera Interface: Look at the bottom left of the screen to hit on the **Menu icon.** ▤

The hidden menu will display all the available advanced effect tools for you to use.

Hit on any of the icons on the menu. It will show the icon and its features on the Camera screen.

The Menu contains:

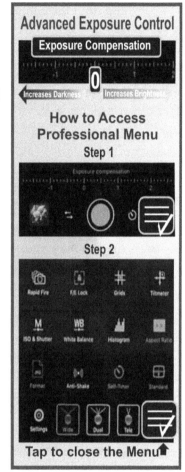

1. Rapid Fire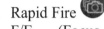
2. F/E (Focus Point and Exposure) Locked
3. Grids
4. Tiltmeter
5. ISO & Shutter
6. White Balance
7. Histogram
8. Aspect Ratio
9. JPEG Format
10. Anti-Shake
11. Self Timer
12. Standard
13. Settings

1. Rapid Fire: The feature of Rapid Fire is the same as the feature of the Burst method of taking many pictures within a very short time by pressing and hold the Shutter.

ProCamera Menu

➢ Hit on the Menu icon

117

- ➤ Hit on the **Rapid Fire** icon
- ➤ Go down to the bottom right of the menu to tap on the Menu icon. This will hide all the menu effect tools.
- ➤ Position your Camera to the Image you want to snap, press, and hold the Shutter to snap the number of shots you want.

2. **Focus Point and Exposure (E/F) Lock:** This feature is used to lock the focus point and exposure level you preferred for the picture.

ProCamera Menu

- ➤ Position your Camera to the image you want to snap.
- ➤ Hit the surface of the Viewfinder for both Focus Point and Exposure Shapes to appear on the screen.
- ➤ On the Viewfinder, you will see focus points in a square shape and exposure in a circular shape. With the use of your finger move the square shape to the area that should be sharp on the viewfinder, and move the circle to the area where the exposure is needed to be corrected.
- ➤ Use the control below to regulate the exposure and the focus as you move your finger on the controlling panel.
- ➤ Hit on the Menu icon at the bottom right of the screen to display the editing tools.
- ➤ Select the F/E Lock icon
- ➤ Hit on the Menu icon at the bottom right to hide the effect tools.
- ➤ Now you can move your Camera anywhere and how to capture different shots without any irregularity.
- ➤ As soon as you have finished taking Photos go to the menu and hit on the **F/E Lock** icon to disable it. The **F/E Lock** icon will appear white when it is disabled but lemon green when it is enabled (active).

Hint: If you move your Camera before you select **F/E Lock** from the Menu the focus and exposure setting will change.

3. **Grids:** The advanced grids are more compact than the grids in the ordinary Camera App. It can be used to centralize a very small image that could not be done with the other grids on the Camera app.

- ➢ Hit on the Menu icon at the bottom right
- ➢ Select **Grids** icon
- ➢ Hit on the Menu icon
- ➢ Use the squares on the viewfinder to set your image.
- ➢ Hit on Shutter to take the Picture.
- ➢ You can go back to Menu to disable the active Grids icon.

4. **Tiltmeter:** This will enable you to balance the Camera of your iPhone. The cross icon shows if the image is correctly positioned.

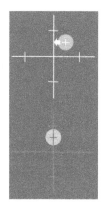

- ➢ Hit on the Menu icon at the bottom right
- ➢ Select **Tiltmeter** icon
- ➢ Hit on the Menu icon
- ➢ Use the Tiltmeter (Big Cross) on the viewfinder to be in line with the small cross and when it is correctly registered on each other the Tiltmeter will turn to **Green**.
- ➢ Hit on Shutter to take the Picture.
- ➢ You can go back to Menu to disable the active Tiltmeter icon.

5. **ISO & Shutter:** This is also called **Manual Mode** that regulates the speed of Shutter and could be used to control exposure as it is used in Digital Single-Len Reflex Camera.

119

The faster the Shutter the more the advantage of producing a clearer picture with low light.

The higher the number of ISO the more light-sensitive your iPhone Camera.

ProCamera Menu

- ➢ Hit on the **Menu icon** at the bottom right
- ➢ Select **ISO & Shutter** icon
- ➢ Hit on the Menu icon
- ➢ At the top of the Viewfinder, you will see Shutter Speed reading rate **1/3xxx s** and **ISO 4x.** Tap on 1/3xxx
- ➢ Use the Shutter Speed to control the speed time.

To Control ISO

- ➢ Hit on the **ISO 4x** (e.g ISO 48) at the top right of the Viewfinder.
- ➢ Drag the **ISO Sensitivity Regulator** below the Viewfinder toward the right to increase your iPhone Camera light sensitivity.

6. **White Balance:** The Picture colors on your Camera are controlled by color temperature which is known as additional Blue that is representing Cooler and additional Yellow which is representing Warmer. If you add more of yellow color to your picture that means it is having additional warming temperature while the increase of Blue color on your picture is reducing the temperature of your picture and the temperature is reading in **Kelvin (K)**

ProCamera Menu

- ➢ Hit on the **Menu** icon at the bottom right
- ➢ Select the **White Balance** icon
- ➢ Hit on the Menu icon
- ➢ At the bottom of the Viewfinder hit on **AWB** the reading scale will show.

> The cooling (Blue) temperature is increasing when you move the Color Temperature Slider toward the left while Warming (Yellow) temperature is increasing when you move the slider toward the right.

Hint: As you are adding blue the temperature reading value will be reducing and as you are adding yellow to the picture the temperature reading value will be increasing.

7. **Histogram**: This is a picture graph that explains the equal exposure level of darkness or brightness pixels on a Picture. It shows if a picture is having high or excessive brightness (i.e. overexposure) or darkness (i.e. underexposure).

ProCamera Menu

> Hit on the **Menu** icon at the bottom right
> Select **Histogram** icon
> Hit on the Menu icon

Hint: The right peak side of the picture exposure graph is representing the maximum brightness pixels in the picture.

The middle area of the picture color graph is showing a minimal level of brightness.

The left peak side of the picture exposure graph is representing the optimal level of darkness.

When you either reduce or add exposure to your picture through the use of Exposure Compensation, It will quickly arrange the histogram to show the effects of the picture color pixels.

For You to Remove the Histograph

> Hit on the **Menu** icon at the bottom right

➤ Hit on the **Histogram** icon to deactivate it. It will change from lemon green to white.
➤ Hit on the Menu icon to minimize the editing tools.

8. **Anti-Shake:** As the name implies, it prevents the image capture from going through an unconscious and uncontrollable shaking defect when the light is low or poor. It ensures clear and sharp capture of images in a poor light environment.

Anti-Shake will automatically switch on itself as soon as the Camera discovered the surrounding light is bad for a good picture. When you launch the **ProCamera App** and go to Menu, you will see the Anti-Shake feature has been automatically switched On to ensure quality Photo.

9. **Aspect Ratio:** This is an interesting ProCamera feature that helps all individuals to print out their photos according to the size of their desirable Photo Frame.

The ratio measures the breadth and height of the Photo you are about to take. By default, you will see 3:2 on your Camera when you have activated the Aspect Ratio option on the menu.

This option is telling you that the size of the Photo breadth will be 3 while the height will be 2.

Practically, if you want to choose a frame, you will need to understand how to work out the Aspect Ratio first.

Ratio 3:2 means, the breadth is taking the size of 3 out of 5 (3/5 or three-fifth) and the height is taking the size of 2 out of 5 (2/5 or two-fifth)

If you are having the size of the frame, you must calculate the ratio between the breath and the height of the frame.

For instance, 4 inches by 6 inches Frame size

In this contest, a small number (4) comes before the bigger number (6). Any of the sides could be considered breadth or height since the difference between them is ratio 3:2.

How can you know that?

Continue dividing both figures with a common number that could go in them until you are unable to divide them again a common number.

Between 4 and 6 the common number for both is 2

Divide both by 2 = 4/2 = 2; and 6/2 = 3

Now you can conclude that the frame is ratio 2:3 is the same as ratio 3:2.

Let's try another frame size 16 inches by 24 inches (16" x 24")

What are the common numbers (also called a common factor) in both?

Start from the smallest number: 2,4, & 8

Those three numbers could completely divide both sides to last the last number that could not allow any division again.

To save time, let's use 8

If you divide both numbers by 8 you will get = 16/8 =2; and 24/8 = 3

The fame 16" x 24" is in Aspect Ratio 2:3.

Therefore, the frame could work perfectly for any picture you have taken with an Aspect Ratio of 3:2

Now, you can try to find out the ratio of these frame sizes.

1. 8" x 12"
2. 32" x 48" and

3. 64" x 96"

I wish you good luck.

You can change the Aspect Ratio from default ratio 3:2 to another commonly available of your own choice by tapping on the **Aspect Ratio** icon in the ProCamera Menu.

Every each time you tap the Aspect Ratio it will change to another option of the ratio which includes:

1. 1:1
2. 3:1 Panorama Size.
3. 4:3
4. 5:4
5. 16:9
6. Golden Mean

10. **File Format:** This will help you to compress your pictures to use very small storage space on your iPhone & iCloud when the pictures are saved in JPG/JPEG format.

Ordinarily, your Camera always saves your Photographs in JPEG format to make them compatible and very useful in all devices.

Although, JPEG pictures are compressed photos, meanwhile, in the process of compressing and saving the pictures in JPEG format they partially lose some degree of light which affects the overall quality. However, they are still pretty good to use.

But, with the use of the **ProCamera App** on your iPhone you can effectively use other options of saving your pictures. The other options are TIFF, RAW, and RAW+JPEG.

These options will not compress your Photos as a result, they will be very heavy and take too much of storage space on your iPhone and iCloud.

The advantage is that any picture you save with either TIFF or RAW will 100% protect the degree of the light, total exposure, and come out excellently.

How to select the File Format of Your Choice

You may want to save a particular picture in a different file format based on a special request. Take the steps below:

ProCamera Menu

> Hit on the **Menu** icon at the bottom right
> Hit on **File Format**, you will first see JPEF; re-tap the icon you will see TIFF and continue tapping it till you see your preferred option.
> Hit on the Menu icon
> When you are through, go back to the menu to reset it to the JPEG file.

CHAPTER SEVEN

All Communication Apps to Express Yourself on Your iPhone

 Some Apps have communication features on your iPhone that could be used to express yourself with others which enable you to pass across information to people that are very important to you and also receive information from them. The Apps will give you access to hear the voice of the caller or record the conversation between both of you.

More so, through the communication app, you can make live text chat with your dearest fellows or colleagues or business partners or family, and instantly receive a reply with the use of cellular data or subscription. Above all, you can make conference audio or video calls with numerous people. The Apps the have the **Communication Features** are:

1. Call App
2. FaceTime App
3. Message App
4. Mail App

The Apps that help in getting more information for communication Apps are:

1. Safari App
2. Siri App
3. iTunes App

The Simple Ways of Calling Different Contacts with Phone App on Your iPhone

The Phone app is one of the most essential primary cores of using the iPhone for communication. The use of the Call App will enable you to rich-out to your people of your through their phone numbers.

The people's phone number could be categorized into two places to separate the most important ones from general ones.

The most inevitable people are considered to be your **Favorites** on the iPhone while others belong to the general **Contacts.** You can assign a separate ringing tone to all contacts in **Favorites.**

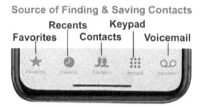

By default, the Phone App is specifically positioned at the base bar of the Homescreen to ease your call making and receiving.

To save your friend contact in Phone app contacts, you will need the phone number, first and last name, email (if available), and picture (if available). But, it is very advisable to save your friend's email in the contact detail because you may need to reach him/her through your Email massage.

Add Contact

Homescreen: Hit on the **Phone App** at the base bar of your iPhone.

Favorites

> Hit on the **Favorite** icon (Star) at the bottom left of the screen.
> Hit on the **Add** icon (Cross) at the top left of your iPhone's screen.
> Go through all contact to locate the named contact or enter the name of the person into the **Search field** to quickly see the **Person's Contact.**
> Hit on the Contact Name
> **Optional Dialog Box:** Hit on the usual way of contacting people such as Message (iMessage or Mail), Call, or FaceTime. For example, select Call.
> Immediately, you will see the selected contact name among **Favorites.**

OR

Homescreen: Hit on the **Phone App** at the base bar of your iPhone.

Contacts

> Hit on **Contacts Icon** at the bottom center of the iPhone's screen.
> Hit on the **search field** to quickly locate the contact's name you are looking for.
> Hit on the contact's name to see all the person's information details, below you will see **Add to Favorites.**
> Hit on the Contact Name
> **Optional Dialog Box:** Hit on the usual way of contacting people such as Message (iMessage or Mail), Call, or FaceTime. For example, select Call.

> Immediately, you will see the selected contact name among **Favorites.**

Remove a Contact from Your iPhone

You need to understand the fact that, whenever you apply to **Delete** command on any contact on your iPhone or Email account, it will completely remove it from your iPhone without a chance of retrieving/restoring it.

Therefore, you have to fully sure about the contact before you hit on **Delete** command.

Homescreen: Hit on **Contacts Icon**

Contacts

> Search for the **Contact's Name** through the search field
> Hit on the exact **Contacts Name**
> Hit on **Edit**
> Move down the screen to hit on **Delete Contacts.**

> For confirmation re-tap on **Delete Contacts** (Confirmatory Dialog Box**).** Immediately the contact will be completely removed from your iPhone Contacts' list.

Set Sorting Order of Contacts List on Your iPhone

The Names of everyone in your Contacts could be arranged in chronological order from A-Z to ease searching for either **First or Second Name.**

You are given the privilege to instruct your iPhone on how you want the name to be arranged, that is if you want the First name to appear before the second the following setting will enable it:

Homescreen: Hit on the **Settings Icon**

Settings: Scroll down to select **Contacts**

Contacts

> **Sort Order:** This will alphabetically arrange either the First or Second Name in Contacts.
> **Display Order**: This will either display the First Name after or before Second Name.

Short Name: Select how the Contact's Name yours will show in Phone, Mail, Messages, FaceTime… and other Apps.

Move Contacts from SIM to iPhone

You can transfer all your contacts on your SIM into your new iPhone if the SIM supports the feature it is very easy to do.

SIM Card Insertion: Insert your SIM containing the contacts you want to transfer into your iPhone.

Homescreen: Hit on the **Settings Icon**

Settings: Hit on **Contacts**

Contacts:

129

- ➤ Move to the middle of the screen to hit on **Import SIM Contacts.**
- ➤ Hit where the contacts should be imported from an optional dialog box that will appear.
- ➤ Hold on till the whole contacts moving process is finished before you proceed.
- ➤ Access your Contact to confirm the complete importation on iPhone.

Hints: iPhone cannot save the contact(s) on SIM card, if you want to transfer contacts from iPhone to iPhone then there will be a need for you to back-up the iPhone with iCloud storage or other transferring means like PC memory, flash, etc.

Activate and Deactivate Contacts for Mail Account

The activation of Contacts will enable you to add contacts in any of your Email Account and the deactivation of Contacts will enable the removal of contact(s) from your iPhone.

Homescreen: Hit **Settings Icon**

Settings: Hit on **Password and Account**

Password and Account: Hit on the **Email Account.**

The Email Account (Gmail/Yahoo): Switch On the **Contacts Activator** to become Green.

To Deactivate Contacts App

The Email Account (Gmail/Yahoo)

- ➤ Switch Off the **Contacts Activator** to become **White.**
- ➤ Hit **Delete from My iPhone.** Immediately the contact will be removed.

Make Your Contacts for Email Account

Homescreen: Hit **Settings Icon**

Settings: Hit on **Password and Account**

130

Password and Account: Hit on **Add Account**

Add Account: Hit on your Email account and switch On **Contacts.**

If you do not have an email account you can hit on **Other** to make Contact Account such as LDAP or CardDAV account is available.

➢ Type your details and password.
➢ Hit on **Next.**

In a situation whereby you are having several accounts set up in the Contacts App and you need a particular account for the contacts:

Homescreen: Hit on **Contacts** App

Contacts: Hit **Groups** at the top left angle of the screen.

Add New Contact to Your Default Account

This is very advisable for you if you are using more than one Email Account in your **Contacts.**

Homescreen: Hit on **Settings Icon**

Settings: Scroll down to select **Contacts**

Contacts: Hit on **Default Account**

Default Account: Select **One** of your **Email Accounts.**

How You Can Make A Call Conveniently

Homescreen: Hit on **Phone App**

Keypad Interface

➢ Type the **Contact Number** if you do not have the person's contact in your iPhone

131

Contact List.
➢ Hit on the **Call Button.** It is the Green Circle.

End Call

➢ The Green Circle Button will change to Red Circle Button, it is called the **End Button.**
➢ Hit the **End Button** to stop the call.

Make A Call from Contacts

Keypad Interface: Look at the bottom center to hit on **Contacts.**

Contacts:

➢ Enter the first-two alphabetical letters that started the name of the person into the search field to speed up the quick discovery of the contact.
➢ Hit on the **Contact's Name**

Contact's Name: Hit on the person's Phone Number.

End Call: Hit the **End Button** to stop the call.

Add People's Phone Number to Your Contact Directly

Keypad Interface

➢ Dial the **Phone Number** of the person correctly.
➢ Hit on **Add to Contact** at the top of the screen.

Request Dialog Box: On a displayed **Request Dialog Box** hit **Create New Contact.**

Create New Contact

➢ Type the First and Second Names

- ➢ Enter the Email of the owner of the Phone Number if you know it (optional).
- ➢ You can choose different **Ringtones** for the contact it is optional.
- ➢ Hit on **Add to Existing Contact**

Add to Existing Contact

- ➢ Look for the **Contact**
- ➢ Enter the Number into the Number text field
- ➢ Hit on **Done.**

Add To Contacts from Recent Called or Received Contacts

You can add the recently ended call phone number into your general Contact by following these steps on your iPhone.

Keypad Interface: Look below and hit **Recents** with a round clock icon.

Recent

- ➢ You will see the recently ended phone number
- ➢ Hit on the **Info icon** in front of the phone number.

Info: Select **Create New Contact**

Create New Contact

- ➢ Type the First and Second Names
- ➢ Enter the Email of the owner of the Phone Number if you know it (optional).
- ➢ You can choose different **Ringtones** for the contact it is optional.
- ➢ Hit on **Add to Existing Contact**

Add to Existing Contact

- ➢ Look for the **Contact**
- ➢ Enter the Number into the Number text field
- ➢ Hit on **Done.**

Now the recent call will appear with the name you used in the adding of the number into your Contacts. The person contact can be found in your overall **Contacts list** on your iPhone.

How to Delete all Recent Contacts

A recent list comprises of the phone numbers of all those you have called, received calls and missed incoming calls, and missed outgoing calls with day and time they were called or received. You can easily remove all the recent history.

Homescreen: Hit on **Phone App Icon**

Keypad Interface: look at the bottom left of the screen and hit on **Recents** (Round Clock Icon).

Recents

> ➢ Look at the top left of the screen hit on **Clear**
> ➢ Hit on the **Clear All Recents** button showing down the screen. If you hit the **Cancel** button, it will reverse the action and the recent list will not be deleted.

All You Can Do When You Are on a Call

1. *You can switch inside speaker to outside Speaker*
2. *You can switch to Video Call.*
3. *You can allow more people to your discussion.*
4. *You can Mute the Voice.*
5. *You can Accept or Decline other incoming calls.*
6. *You can compose a message to reply to your call.*
7. *You can make use of Remind Me to program a reminder for you to return the call of the caller later.*
8. *You can search through apps (e.g. Mail, Photo, Note, Calendar, Safari, Social Media) to get relevant information. Browsing Apps will require a Wi-Fi network connection on your iPhone.*

How to Allow or Prevent Call When You Are On A Call

To Accept Call: On the calling, the interface slides the Call button toward the right to answer the call.

To Prevent the Call and Forward It into Voicemail: Double-click the **Switch Button** at the right side of the iPhone.

Send Message To Caller: Hit on the **Message Icon** to text messages and send them to your caller.

Use Reminder To Recall: You can hit on **Remind Me** to instruct reminding me to call the caller after you stop the current call.

How You Can Make Your Voicemail Active

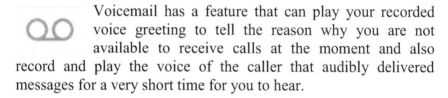 Voicemail has a feature that can play your recorded voice greeting to tell the reason why you are not available to receive calls at the moment and also record and play the voice of the caller that audibly delivered messages for a very short time for you to hear.

You can also choose a greeting out of some default recorded greetings for your outgoing greeting.

To make Voicemail to be active you have to go into the Setting or through Voicemail Icon in the Phone app to Set Up your **Password and Greeting**.

Homescreen: Hit on the **Phone App** icon.

Keypad Interface: below the screen hit on **Voicemail Icon** at the last bottom left.

Voicemail: Hit on **Set Up Now.**

Password

> ➤ Type in the **Voicemail Password** that must be in 4-digit.
> ➤ Retype the same **Voicemail Password** to confirm your consistency.

Greeting

- ➢ Hit on **Custom** options to make your outgoing greeting with your voice or otherwise.
- ➢ Hit on **Record** to start. (Say your greeting as you want it to be said).
- ➢ Hit on **Stop** to end the recording.
- ➢ Hit on **Play** to hear your recorded greeting.
- ➢ If you are not okay, you can re-tap the **Record.**
- ➢ If you are okay then hit on **Save**

How to Reset Voicemail Set Up Through Settings

Homescreen: Hit on the **Settings icon.**

Settings: Select **Phone App**

Phone: Hit on **Change Voicemail Password**

Password

- ➢ Hit on **New Password**
- ➢ Type in the **Previous Password**
- ➢ Type in the **New Password**
- ➢ Hit on **Done.**

How to Listening to Your Voicemail

 If you are having calls that have been forwarded into Voicemail, you will see the notification number of new Voicemails at the top-right edge side of the **Voicemail Icon** at the last bottom left of the keypad interface.

Homescreen: Hit on the **Phone App** icon.

Keypad Interface: below the screen hit on **Voicemail Icon** at the last bottom left.

Voicemail

➤ Hit on **Message**

➤ Hit on **Play** to hear the recorded caller's voice.

➤ Hit on **Call Back** to replay the voice message.

➤ If you are satisfied with the message you can hit on Delete.

To Call the Voicemail

Homescreen: Hit on the **Phone App** icon.

Keypad Interface: below the screen hit on **Voicemail Icon** at the last bottom left.

Voicemail:

➤ Hit on **Call Voicemail.**
➤ Hit on the **End Button.**

Send Junks and Unwanted Callers into Voicemail

This is will only allow the saved contacts on your iPhone to ring-out but unknown contacts will be sent to Voicemail

Homescreen: Hit on the **Settings icon.**

Settings: Tap on **Phone**

Phone: Hit on the **Salience Unknown Caller** activator to become Green.

Set Call Waiting in Settings

Wi-Fi Network connection is very important to make Wi-Fi call active in Dual SIM. You will see Call Waiting when one line call is active and another incoming call occurs in another line.

Homescreen: Hit on **Settings**

Settings: Hit on **Phone App**

Phone: Select **Call Waiting** and hit on the activator to become Green. Make Home Swipe Up

How to Select Special Sound & Hepatic Rings for Calls, Messages, Alert, & Mail Notifications

You can assign separate ringtones to different contacts in iPhone Contacts. You may consider giving similar ringtone and vibration to all the contacts in Favorite and different ringtones to some set of people in all Contacts.

You can use ringtone to know when closed family members in the Favorites are calling and when your important business partners are calling.

Homescreen: Hit on **Settings**

Settings: Hit on **Sound & Hepatics**

Sound & Hepatics

> ➢ Hit on the **Vibrate on Ring** activator to turn Green
> ➢ Hit on the **Vibrate on Silence** activator to turn Green
> ➢ Select your **Ringtone** and choose any of the default Ringtones available.

Make Special Ringtone for Individual Contact

Homescreen: Hit on the **Contact App** icon

Contacts

> ➢ Search for contact through the search field.
> ➢ Hit on the **Contact**
> ➢ Hit on **Edit**
> ➢ Hit on **Ringtone**
> ➢ Select one of the **Default Ringtones**.

Make **Home Swipe Up**.

CHAPTER EIGHT

How To Fully Enjoy Apple TV, FaceTime App, Message App, Mail App, Safari App, & Siri on Your iPhone

How to Watch Apple TV and Perform Online Activities at the Same Time

Apple TV is more improved in the latest iPhone 12 Mini, 12, 12 Pro, and 12 Pro Max.

Although you might have been familiarized with the use of Apple TV still I will need to take you a little further to enjoy the innovativeness added to the Apple TV modification through some simple steps for the sake of the beginner.

In iOS 14, you could be watching your Apple TV while you are doing some other things like browsing, chatting, editing, mailing others, or performing online activities on your iPhone.

You could conveniently minimize the size of the Apple TV to appear portable on your iPhone screen.

How to be watching Apple TV while doing other things on the iPhone

Homescreen: Hit on Apple TV App to open the interface of the TV screen.

Apple TV Screen: Look at the top left of the Apple TV screen to tap on **Minimize Icon**.

Immediately, the TV screen will minimize; then, use your finger to move the TV screen to anywhere

139

you prefer it to be on the iPhone screen.

You can continue watching your Apple TV and at the same time be working on your iPhone.

How You Could Perfectly Use FaceTime App to Make Video Calls, & Conference Calls with Customized Animoji

 FaceTime App is an interactive method of communicating with those who are using iPhones and their contact details are on your iPhone Contacts.

It has a unique video communication feature that can enable you to see the face of the person you are calling or the person that called you.

Most of the time, it is important that you first and foremost send a request to the person you want to make a FaceTime video call with on either an interactive iMessages interface or through an audio call that you will like to make or switch to FaceTime Video Call.

You have to ensure that the persons are using the iPhone and you are having enough Wi-Fi Data to make the call.

You can also use FaceTime to make Conference Video Call with other iPhone users in your contacts but you must notify those that will participate in the conference call on text message interface the time, the reason for the group discussion, and ask each of them if they will be available.

Make FaceTime Set Up in Settings to be Active

Homescreen: Hit on **Settings Icon**

Settings: Scroll down to select **FaceTime**

FaceTime

> ➢ Put On the **FaceTime** Activator to become Green

140

- ➢ Put On the **FaceTime Live Photo** Activator to become Green
- ➢ Provide your **Phone Number**
- ➢ Provide your **Apple ID**
- ➢ Provide your **Email Add** (Optional)

Make FaceTime Audio Calls or Video Call

Homescreen: Hit on **FaceTime Icon**

FaceTime: Hit on **Add Contact** at the top right of the screen.

Contact: Use the search field to quickly get the contact.

Audio Call: Hit on the **Audio Call button** to fix the audio call.

 OR

Video Call: Hit on the **Video Call button** to fix the video call.

How to Change from Normal Audio Calls to FaceTime Video Call

On the calling interface, you will see an option of using FaceTime Video

Video Call: Hit on the **Video Call button** to fix a video call .

Hit on the **End button** at the lower left of the FaceTime Video call interface.

How You Can Change from Text Message Interaction to FaceTime Call

Homescreen: Hit on **Messages App Icon**

141

Message

> Hit on the **Compose icon** at the top right of the screen.

> Type the name of the person you want to chat with into the **"To"** Search field.
> During the live iMessage chatting with your friend, hit on the name of your friend at the top center of the screen to choose FaceTime.
> Hit on **FaceTime Icon**
> Choose either **Audio or Video Call**
> Hit on the End button to end the FaceTime call

How to Make Multiple Live Chat

Homescreen: Hit on **Messages App Icon**

Messages

> Hit on the **Compose icon** at the top right of the screen.

> Type the **Names or Phone Number or Email Add** of all persons you want to chat with into the **"To"** Search field. For example, *Hannah Berm, Daniel Rose, Dan Floral*
> Below the screen hit the text message field for **Keyboard** to show-up, type your text message, and hit on the **Send** icon to deliver your message into the chat interface.

How to Change the Group Conference Conversation to FaceTime Video Call

It is the same step of moving from a single chat that you will take to change your communication mode to FaceTime Video or Audio Call.

Message (Chatting Page)

> Hit on the names of your friends at the top center of the screen to choose **FaceTime**.

142

- ➢ Hit on **FaceTime Icon**
- ➢ Choose either **Audio or Video Call**
- ➢ Hit on the End button to end the FaceTime call

How to Replace Your Face with Animoji during FaceTime Video

Homescreen: Launch **FaceTime** App

FaceTime

- ➢ On the FaceTime, Call interface hit on the **Video Call button.**
- ➢ Hit on **Effect Button.** ✿
- ➢ Hit on either **Memoji** or **Animoji** available 🐵
- ➢ Scroll toward the right or left to choose.
- ➢ Hit on your preferred Memoji or Animoji. Immediately your face will be replaced with the chosen Memoji or Animoji.
- ➢ To remove the Memoji or Animoji hit on **Cancel** ✕ and your face reappear normally.

If you want to change the current Memoji or Animoji: Restart all over from the beginning of the above process and reselect the new Memoji of Animoji of your choice.

Other Ways of Using Message App on Your iPhone

You can majorly use Messages App to make a direct live chat with those who are in your iPhone contacts using iPhone through iMessage.

Also, you can use it to send a text message to those who are in your contacts using Android.

How to Compose and Reply Text Messages

Homescreen: Hit on **Messages App Icon**

> Hit on the **Compose icon** at the upper right of the screen.

> Type the name of the person you want to chat with into the "**To**" Search field.

OR

> If you want to reply to any received message in the massage App, hit on the particular message. It will launch you into the compose text message interface.
> Hit the text field to type your text message.
> Hit the **Send Button,** that is, the Blue Send Button is for iMessage ⬆ while Green Send Button is for SMS ⬆.

Your iPhone will automatically determine if the text message is iMessage or SMS. Once you see the blue button showing for sending your text message that implies you are about to send iMessage to the person using iPhone but if it shows green that means, you are sending text SMS to an Android user.

How to add Emoji to your Text Message

> At the lower left side of the Keyboard hit on **Emoji** Icon
> You may scroll up and down or right side to select by tapping on anyone you like.
> Hit on the Send button to move it into the chat interface.

How to add Effects to your Text Message

> At the immediate left side of the Keyboard Text Field, you will see **App Store** Icon, hit on it
> Select the **Animoji icon** at the bottom roll menu 🐵 .
> You will see different **Animoji** images.

- Select Animoji you like and position it within the square view guide. Once the Animoji is registered, it will be mimicking your face and mouth movement.
- Hit on **Recording Button** at the bottom right side of the view frame to start recording your audio voice with Animoji.
- Hit on the same button to stop the recording and change the button to the **Send** button. It will replay itself for you to hear.
- If you are satisfied then hit on the **Send button** to forward the Animoji into the **Chat** interface for the person you are chatting with to receive and access.
- You can still reselect another Animoji below by scrolling through the arranged Animoji drawer and hit on another different Animoji to make a new recording.
- If you are not satisfied hit on the **Delete** button at the upper right.

For Additional Effects

- You can still go-ahead to get more Animoji in the App Store by tapping on the **App Store** icon at the lower-left corner of the screen and hit on **View Apps.**
- You can still search for "**Images**" that are very accurate to your message by tapping on the **Search Icon** below.
- Hit on Find Images Field showing above the displayed images.
- Enter the types of images you are looking for like Thinking, Disagreement, Excitement, Sleeping, Busy, Hungry, Disturbed, Listening, Working… and many others. You may pick from the appearing keywords as you are entering the word.
- There is also a **Free Hand Drawing icon** that could allow you to draw anything you like and send it to the person you are chatting with.

145

> ➤ You can also send home videos through **YouTube, Audio Music, Recents Selfie Pictures/other Pictures, or Video** through Camera.

How to Make Your Customized Animoji or Memoji on Your iPhone

Messages

> ➤ At the immediate left side of the Keyboard Text Field, you will see **App Store** Icon, hit on it.
> ➤ Select the **Animoji icon** at the bottom roll menu .
> ➤ Scroll toward right hit on Add/Cross Sign for **New Memoji**
> ➤ Select **Skin** and adjust it with the available set of colors and remove face spots by choosing freckles.
> ➤ Select **Hairstyle** to choose either male hairstyle or female hairstyle
> ➤ Move to **Head Shape** to select the loveliest chin.
> ➤ Move to the **Eye** section to pick the type of eye you like having on your Memoji.
> ➤ Continue to select all the parts of the face of your Memoji from the other options including **Browse, Nose & Lips, Ear** with different pretty earing, **Facial Hair** with either Mustard & Beard or Sideburns, **Eyewear** like glasses, and **Headwear** like face-caps, hat, etc., till you complete achieve a beautiful looking Memoji. It is a creative place that is full of fun.
> ➤ As soon as you are satisfied with your **Self Making Memoji** then hit on **Done** to save the Memoji and include it with the group of Animoji.

You can use your Memoji to make a FaceTime video call or iMessage audio chat on the Message App interface of your iPhone.

How to Add Animation Effect to Your Key Text Message

Messages

- Type your short text message into the text field. For example, *Stay Home Safe, Drink Responsibly, Daily Exercise Importance, Let's Jubilate, Today's Plan, etc.*
- Press down the **Send** button for a while to launch **Effect Page** contains:
  - ✓ **Bubble Animation Effects:** Slam, Loud, Gentle and Invisible Ink.
  - ✓ **Screen Animation Effects:** Send with Echo, Send with Confetti, Send with Spotlight… and others.

Send with Effect

- At the upper center of the page, you will see **Bubble & Screen.**
- Hit one of the various effects menu to know the best. Once you have known the best effect, leave it on the option.
- Hit on the **Screen** option above.
- Swipe the screen from right to left to see the various screen effects. When you have seen the most suitable **Screen Effect** for your Text message then hit on the **Send** button.
- If you are not satisfied then hit on the **Cancel** button to return to the message interface.

How to Send Voice Message

This makes the message easy for those who are not having enough time to chat or who are not very fast a typing text messages to quickly deliver their messages, as a result, they choose a short audio recording message that is précised, specific, and facts.

Messages

- Go to the bottom left of the keyboard and hit on **Microphone Icon.**
- Start an audio message. You will see the linear sound wave of your voice as you are talking. The louder your voice the larger the width of the sound wave.
- As soon as you finished the audio message the hit **Send** button above.
- It will be seen in the chat interface.

> ➤ Look at the bottom left of the screen and hit on the Keyboard icon to return the Keyboard.

Hint: You can also dictate your message to Siri that is capable of changing all your audio dictation messages to text messages and sent it to the right contact you commanded.

How to Efficiently Use Mail App to Get Good Results

Mail app is an avenue to receive and send a message(s) with the use of Electronic Mail (Email) Service Providers which include **Google** (...@gmail.com), **Yahoo** (...@ yahoo.com), **iCloud** (...@icloud.com), **Outlook.com** (...@outlook.com)... and many others.

The use of the Mail App will fully allow you to receive or send documents to loved ones and business associates. It is more officially use for a better transaction between you and other business organizations.

Mail has become the most reliable acceptable official interactive platform to provide your vital details and execution of online obligations.

Therefore, the essential processes for you to become a wonderful beneficiary user of Mail great opportunities.

There are channels through which you can get information that can be added to your composed message such addition is called **Document Attachment.**

You can save documents with any **Microsoft Office** format or you may directly go to a website to copy very relevant information that is helpful to clarify your message and subsequently paste it within your message.

If you already have two or more email accounts and you want to add them to your new iPhone there are some simple steps you have to do in your iPhone Settings.

To make Mail effectively functional, then you have to carry-out either manual or automatic setup in Settings on your iPhone.

How to Put Manual Set Up for Mail App in Place

The manual is simply designed for those who are using different Emails from the suggested email accounts on the Add Account Interface. Then, the **Other** is the correct option to choose.

Homescreen: Hit on the **Settings** icon.

Settings: Move down and select **Accounts & Passwords.**

Accounts & Passwords: Hit on **Add Account**

Add Account: Look at the lower region of the screen and hit on **Other.**

Other: Hit on **Add Mail Account**

New Account

- ➢ Type your **Name**
- ➢ Type your specific **Email Account**
- ➢ Type your **Password**
- ➢ Type your **Description**
- ➢ Hit on **Next** for the setup to be finalized and the Mail will search for your Email Account.
- ➢ Once the searching is successful

149

then hit on **Done.**

If the Email Account Settings could not be found by Mail then do the following to roundup the setup.

Second Phase New Account: If you do not know your Email settings ask your email service provider to tell you if the email settings belong to IMAP or POP. As soon as, you confirm

> ➢ Hit on **IMAP/POP**
> ➢ Provide details on **INCOMING & OUTCOMING MAIL SERVER**
>> ✓ **Host Name**
>> ✓ **User Name & Password**
> ➢ Hit on **Next** at the top.
> ➢ Once your details are accurate then hit **Save**

Your inability to provide the correct details will lead to the inability to complete the manual setup.

How to Put Automatic Set Up for Mail App in Place

Homescreen: Hit on the **Settings** icon.

Settings: Move down and select **Accounts & Passwords.**

Accounts & Passwords: Hit on **Add Account**

Add Account: Select your Email service source (e.g. Yahoo).

Yahoo

> ➢ Type your existing **Yahoo Address**
> ➢ Type correct **Password**

(If you want to look into your email account then you can hit on **Sign In**, when you are through, then **Sign Out** to return to the previous Set Up page because you still have some tasks to complete. Better still, complete the tasks before you Sign-In into your account).

➢ Hit on **Next** to continue and hold on for the processing to complete.

In Your Yahoo Account (...@yahoo.com)

➢ Switch On the **Activator** of the following applications **Contacts App, Mail Contacts, Calendar App, Note App & Reminder App.**
➢ The upper right region of the screen hit on **Save.**

How to Activate the Function of Essential Tools for Message Composition

All essential tools for a perfect write up and excellent message composition should be activated in the Settings to ensure correct spellings, arrangement, capitalization... and many others**.**

Homescreen**:** Hit on the **Settings icon**

Settings: Select **General**

General: Select **Keyboards**

Keyboards: Switch On the following **Activation buttons** of **Auto-Capitalization, Auto-Correction, Check Spelling, Enable Caps Lock, Predictive, Smart Punctuation, Character Preview, Shortcut, and Enable Dictation.**

To Change Your Keyboard to One-Handed Keyboard

On the same Keyboards page

Keyboards: Select **One-Handed Keyboard** and hit on the **Activator**

151

OR

You can also get the selection of One-Handed Keyboard directly on the Mail to compose page.

Homescreen: Hit on **Mail App**

Mail: Hit the **Compose icon** at the top right region of the screen or

select received Email and later hit on compose or reply icon.

New Message

> ➤ Hit the front of "To:" for the text cursor to show and the Keyboard to show below.
> ➤ At the lower region of the Keyboard in the new message interface, press down the Earth icon for different types of Keyboard to show.
> ➤ Hit on either left or right-hand side Keyboard that is very convenient for you.

How to Write and Send Email Messages

Homescreen: First and foremost, go to the **Control Center** to put On Wi-Fi Network and hit on **Mail App**

Mail: Hit Compose Icon at the top right region of the screen or

select received Email and later hit on compose or reply icon.

New Message

> ➤ Hit the front of "To:" for the text cursor to show and the Keyboard to show below.
> ➤ Type the **Name or Email Address** of the receiving contact (the person's or company's email address).
> ➤ Hit the front of "**Subject:**" to type a short theme of your message.

152

➤ Hit on the text field interface to start writing your text message. Once you are through then hit on the **Send icon** at the top right region of the screen .

➤ How to Directly Get Name or Email from Your iPhone Contact

You can directly get the name or email address of the person you want to send an email message to through the Contacts on your iPhone.

New Message: Hit on the **Add/Cross** icon to launch Contacts and use the search field to quickly locate the contact you are looking for.

How to Attach Document to Your Message

It is advisable to attach a PDF or JPEG document to your Email because the document cannot be altered.

Mail: Hit Compose Icon at the top right region of the screen or select received Email and later hit on compose or reply icon.

New Message: After you have entered the above "**To**" info (name or email add of where you are sending a message), **Subject and** You have composed your message.

➤ Press down anywhere on the message field for **Edit Menu** to show.

➤ Hit on the **Arrow** at the end of the **Edit menu** to select **Add Attachment.**

➤ It will open to your iPhone document storage and iCloud Drive. Navigate through the App you used such as **Pages App, Keynotes App...** and others.

For Photo or Video

➢ You can also attach pictures to your message by tapping or press down the field and be tapping on the arrow at the end till you will see **Insert Photo** or **Video.**

> ✓ It will launch out your Photo library to select your **Pictures.** Carefully navigate through the exact category you have your pictures.
> ✓ Hit on your **Pictures** and **Send** them to upload on your massage field.

Copy Information from Website

> ✓ In the down middle of the iPhone Notch slide-down a little to see the App browsing text field.
> ✓ Enter Safari, you will see the App and hit on it to access the web page.
> ✓ Enter web add, highlight the massage, and hit copy.
> ✓ Go to the base of the horizontal bar and swipe from the left end to the right end. You will see the New Message page.
> ✓ Hit the place you want to paste the copied info to display on the message field for the edit menu to show an option of **Paste.** Hit Paste and what you copied will display.

OR

Homescreen: Hit on Safari to launch the web add text field.

> ✓ Copy your message as explained above.
> ✓ Move your finger from the middle bottom of the iPhone in inverted seven Γ to see the minimized **New Message Page**. (go to **Guide Four** learn "How to see reduced app pages")
> ✓ Hit on the New Message Page and follow the above pasting steps.

➢ Once you are through with all the documents attachments, then hit on **Send** ⬆.

All You Can Ask Siri To Do For You Through Voice Dictation

 Siri features will help you to organize and properly program your daily, weekly, monthly, and yearly activities successfully.

It is a unique tool iPhone that can help you to operate all the applications on your iPhone quickly and easily. Siri can help you activate any app or control on your iPhone.

Siri can supply you with all current information happening around the world; it could tell you the climatic condition as the moment, traffic condition, reminding you of every important saved event in your organizer or calendar.

Siri could help you set an alarm when you ask it to do so. It can change your dictated message to a text message and send it to the instructed contact. It can translate the English language to any other language like French, German, Spanish... and more others.

It can help you locate a place on a Google map and show you the bearing compass to get the place. It can assist you to find out a review or reputation about an organization or person.

Siri can tell you where you can locate your favorites using iPhone that you have already registered with Siri. It could help you forward calls to your acquainted favorites or anyone in your contact... among many other benefits.

When you call Siri, you will hear a human voice that could be a female or male voice. It depends on the types of sex voice you choose during Siri Setup.

However, for you to know all that Siri could do on your iPhone for you.

Siri Language Translation

A complete guide about the full steps on how to use Siri for language translation has been discussed in *Chapter 5.*

How You Can Effectively Make Siri To Serve You

For Siri to work on your iPhone you must first and foremost finish the setup in the settings, if you have not done it during the iPhone Automatic Setup or Manual Setup.

Homescreen: Hit on **Settings**

Settings: Move down to select **Siri & Search**

Siri & Search: Put On all the below **Activation Buttons** and select your preferable features for each option.

> ➢ Listen for "Hey Siri".
> ➢ Press Side Button for Siri.
> ➢ Allow Siri When Locked.
> ➢ Language.
> ➢ Siri Voice.
> ➢ Voice Feedback.
> ➢ My Information.
> ➢ **SIRI SUGGESTIONS**
>> ✓ Suggestion in Search
>> ✓ Suggestions in Lock Up

Lock Screen or Homescreen:

> ➢ Unlock the iPhone (If you did not activate " When Locked")
> ➢ Press the Switch, Sleep, or Wake Button on the right side of your iPhone. (If you have activated "Press Side Button for Siri")
> ➢ **Say,** Hey Siri! What can Siri do
> ➢ Siri will respond and show you all things that it could do.

You can also use Apple Earpods to call the attention of Siri

> ➢ Click the Answering middle button to call Siri's attention.

➢ Say Hey Siri!
➢ Immediately Siri will answer you. Siri is very sensitive to "Hey Siri", and then continue with your question.

How You Can Perfectly Use Safari App

 Safari App on your iPhone makes use of Cellular Service and Wi-Fi Network Data to facilitate the efficiency, however, without network and data you cannot access Safari App.

The use of the Safari app will give the privilege of visiting many websites and move from a webpage to another webpage to gather several details or facts online.

Safari suggests a more related website that you can get more useful messages and also display all the favorite websites.

You can download or save apps through the Safari browser on your iPhone into My iPhone or iCloud drive. The Safari browsing window is loaded with many beneficial tools like:

➢ **Page Icon:** To move from webpage to another webpage ▢
  ✓ **Add New Tab (Add Icon** ┼**)** to add more **Tab**
  ✓ **Private** to open a confidential browsing window.
  ✓ **Close Icon** to delete the page at the top left edge ✕
  ✓ **Done**
➢ **Share Icon** to send a page to other apps like Mail, Message, Add to Notes, Bookmark, Reading List, etc.; or to social media page which will be displayed the options of where you can save the webpage. Check any of the below options to determine what format the document will be sent:
  ✓ **Automatic:** It will select the exact appropriate format for every application or action
  ✓ **PDF**
  ✓ **Web Archive**

- ➤ **Download Icon** to access the recent download files on Safari. ⊕
- ➤ **URL with A Small and A Big (AA)**: Small A is used to reduce the font size and the big A is to increase the font size. It is designed to enable the following settings:
  - ✓ Small A Font Size Settings
  - ✓ Big A Size Settings
  - ✓ Show Reader View ▯
  - ✓ Hide Toolbar ↖
  - ✓ Request Desktop Website ⬛
  - ✓ Website Settings ⊘

How to Put the Safari Settings in Place

Homepage: Hit on **Settings**.

Settings: Scroll down the screen and hit on **Safari**

Safari

- ➤ **SEARCH**
  Allow Safari to access Siri by tapping on **Siri & Search** and Activate the switch.
- ➤ **SEARCH**
  - ✓ **The Search Engine** will select your preferable source e.g. Google.
  - ✓ Put On the **Searching Engine Suggestions** Activator.
  - ✓ Put On the **Safari Suggestions** Activator.
  - ✓ Hit on **Quick Website Search** to select **On**
  - ✓ Put On the **Preload Top Hit** Activator.
- ➤ **GENERAL**
  - ✓ Activate **Autofill**
  - ✓ Put On the **Frequency Visited Sites** Activator.
  - ✓ Put On the **Favorite** Activator
  - ✓ Hit on **Favorites** to select **Favorites**
  - ✓ Put On the **Block Pop-up** Activator
  - ✓ Put On the **Show Link Previews** Activator

- ✓ Hit on **Download** to select the storage source e.g. My iPhone and iCloud.
- ➢ **TABS**
  - ✓ Put On **Show Tab Bar** Activator
  - ✓ If you want Icons to be shown in the Tab then you may put On **Show Icons in Tabs'** activation button.
  - ✓ Hit on **Open Links** to select **In New Tab**
  - ✓ Hit on **Close Tabs** to select when you want the open tabs to be closed automatically by Safari. (e.g. Manually, After One Day, After One Week, or After One Month).
- ➢ **PRIVACY & SECURITY**
  - ✓ Put On **Prevent Cross-Site Tracking** activator.
  - ✓ Do not activate **Block All Cookies** because they cannot transmit viruses and your iPhone details cannot be hacked by network hackers.
  - ✓ Put On **Fraudulent Websites Warning'**s activator
  - ✓ Put On **Check for Apple Pay** activator: it will enable you to if the Apple Pay activated and if you are having an Apple Account.
- ➢ **Clear History and Website Data:** If you hit this option you will be able to clear all the browsing history and website data on your iPhone.
- ➢ **SETTING FOR WEBSITE**
  - ✓ Hit on **Page Zoom** for selection between 50%-300% but you may choose 100% for the normal setting.
  - ✓ Hit on **Request Desktop Website** for a selection of Websites.
  - ✓ Hit on **Reader** for selection
  - ✓ Hit on **Camera** for selection of Image Size.
  - ✓ Hit on **Microphone** for selection
- ➢ **READING LIST**
  - ✓ You can activate **Automatically Save Offline** if you want all reading lists in the iCloud to be automatically saved.
  - ✓ Hit on **Advance** for selection.

How To Start Safari Browsing Benefit on Your iPhone

Homescreen: Hit on **Safari Icon** at the lower bar menu of the page.

Safari:

- ➢ Hit on the **Browsing Text Field** to type in your searching words from the appeared keyboard.
  - ✓ You may select from the predictive dropdown keywords.
  - ✓ You may also type your **web address** directly if you are very sure about it.
- ➢ Hit on the **"Go"** button on your keyboard and what you are looking for will come up.

  If you are searching for social media applications like Facebook, WhatsApp… and many others then hit on the app or hit on the download option if you want to download on your iPhone.

  For **Webpage**: Once the page is displayed "you want to save the page as **Bookmark** for future or reference purpose".
  - ✓ Hit on **Bookmark Icon** at the bottom of the page.

  - ✓ Select **Add Bookmark for 3 Tabs** on the informative dialog box to **Save** it inside a **New Folder.**
  - ✓ **New Folder:** Give the **Web Tab** a Name, hit on **Done** and it will be saved in the Favorite browsing tabs.
  - ✓ If you want to open the web tab later. Hit on Bookmark and select the Name of the web tab and the page will open.

- ➢ **About Favorites:** These are the websites you visit often and automatically displayed below your Safari browsing search field.
  - ✓ You can just hit on any of the come web icons to directly launch the webpage of the website without you retyping the website address into the search field machine.
  - ✓ It is very easy and pretty cool to use.
  - ✓ If still want to open another website, all you need to do is to hit on **Add New Tab** Icon at the right bottom of the screen. ⊥
  - ✓ A new page with your favorite websites will be displayed then hit on the other website to also launch another webpage for you to access easily.
- ➢ **Move From Tab Page To Tab Page**
  - ✓ Hit on the Switch Page Icon at the last right bottom of the screen.
  - ✓ You will see all the open pages filed up behind one another. With the help of your finger slightly swipe down to reselect any of the pages by tapping on the page.
  - ✓ **Delete Tab Page:** Look at the top left edge of each page you will see **Cancel Icon**, tap on it and the tab page will be deleted.
- ➢ **Other Places You Can Save Your Place** ⬆
  - ✓ Hit on the **Share Icon** to access the various apps that you can choose and save the web tap, as mentioned above.
- ➢ **Use Share Icon to Transfer Webpage from Your iPhone to Another Apple Device** ⬆
  - ✓ Go to the bottom of the page and hit on the **Share icon.**
  - ✓ Select on **AirDrop** Icon
  - ✓ Locate the Apple device **Name** and select. On the other Apple device hit **Accept** on the informative dialog box; instantly you will see the **Webpage** on the other Apple device screen.

161

What You Can Do When Webpage Is Not Loading on Safari or Safari Not Responding

There are major technical problems that could prevent Safari from not responding or failed to load the webpage.

1. **Wi-Fi Network:** First and foremost ensure that there is an effective network of Wi-Fi connection on your iPhone.
   - ✓ **Problem 1:** If your Wi-Fi network is perfectly connected and there is no visible network indication on your iPhone.
   - ✓ **Solution 1:** Relocate yourself to a place where you can see the Wi-Fi network because the stronger the Wi-Fi network the more Safari will be efficiently responding to the loading webpage.

How to Reactivate the Wi-Fi Network in Setting

Homescreen: Hit on **Settings Icon**

Settings: Select **Wi-Fi**

Wi-Fi: Put Off the **Wi-Fi** Activator 40secs and re-put it On. Go back to Settings and select **Mobile Data.**

Mobile Data: Put Off the **Mobile Data** Activator for a 40secs and re-put it On. Go back to Settings and select **General**

General: Select **Reset**

Reset

➢ Select **Reset Network Settings**
➢ Hit on the **Enter Password** that will show below.

Enter Password: Type in the **Password** and confirm the **Safari.**

✓ **Problem 2:** If you are having s strong Wi-Fi network and Safari is not responding or loading a webpage.

✓ **Solution 2:** Crosscheck the Safari settings as some had been stated above and while the rest will be discussed below under **Settings.**

2. **Settings Crosschecking:** Initially go through all the Safari Settings above. Move a little further by tapping on **Advanced** to confirm the various activations of Safari Settings.

Homescreen: Hit on **Settings Icon**

Settings: Scroll down to select **Safari**

Safari: Start verifying the activated buttons one by one till you get to **Advanced**. Hit on the **Advanced.**

Advanced: Hit on each activation button to put Off and put On again. If you have not activated the below features on your iPhone before ensure that you activate them all because they are very important.

✓ **Advanced:** Initially turn Off the feature one by one to confirm the Safari response, if it is working fine. But, if it is not yet responding put On the feature and repeat the same action on the next feature till you get the one that is responsible for the Safari abnormality.

- Re-put On the **JavaScript** activation button.
- Select **Experimental Features.**

✓ **Experimental WebKit Features**
- Turn Off & Turn On **Blank anchor target implies...** activation button.
- Turn Off & Turn On **Fetch API Request KeepAlive ...** activation button.
- Turn Off & Turn On **Quirk to prevent delayed initial pain...** activation button.
- Turn Off & Turn On **Intersection Observer...** activation button.

163

- Turn Off & Turn On **Media Capabilities Extensions** activation button.
- Turn Off & Turn On **Pointer Events** activation button.
- Re-put On **Swap Processes on Cross-Site...** activation button.
- Turn Off & Turn On **Synthetic Editing Commands** activation button.
- Turn Off & Turn On **Block top-level redirects by third...** activation button.
- Turn Off & Turn On **Visual Viewport API** activation button.
- Turn Off & Turn On **WebRTC H264 Simulcast** activation button.
- Turn Off & Turn On **WebRTC mDNS ICE Candidates** activation button.
- Turn Off & Turn On **WebRTC Unified Plan** activation button.
- Turn Off & Turn On the **WebRTC VP8** activation button.
- Turn Off & Turn On **Disable Web SQL** activation button

CHAPTER NINE

How to Improve Your Security Apple ID, Face ID, and Passcode after iPhone Setup

How to Create a Reliable Apple ID on Your iPhone

A perfect technical Apple ID (Identity) provides absolute security for your newly owned iPhone and Apple Pay Credit Card. You can use Apple Pay Credit Card to buy more interesting applications, or pay flight fees; and to get more free games, activation of important features on your iPhone you will need the Apple ID.

If you create an Apple ID on your iPhone, it will enable you to link all the later purchased Apple devices like Apple iPhones, iPods, Macbook, iMac, Mac, and Watch together. That is if you are privileged to have more than one same or different types of Apple devices.

How To Create Your Apple ID Process

1. **Homescreen** Approach the Settings Icon by hitting on it.
2. **Settings:** Look at the side of Profile Picture at the top and hit on **Sign In to Your iPhone.**
3. **Apple ID**
   - ➢ In the Email text field, type your active **Email Address**.
   - ➢ Look at the top right angle of the screen to tap on **Next.**
   - ➢ Hit on an option of **Don't Have An Apple ID**
   - ➢ You will see an informative box with **Create Apple ID.** Tap on the option.
4. **Date of Birth**
   - ➢ Type in your **Date of Birth** in the provided text field.
   - ➢ At the top angle of the screen hit on **Next.**

5. **Name:** Provide your **Name and Last Name** into the text field and hit on **Next.**

6. Email
   ➤ Make sure you enter the initial **Email** without a typographical mistake or choose to **Get Free iCloud Email Address** and hit on the **Next** option.
   ➤ If you choose **Free iCloud Email** tap on **Next** and **Continue.**
   Password
   ➤ You will be allowed two times to type your **Password.** Type the same password in the first password text field into the second verify password text field. If incorrect it won't continue.
   ➤ Make eight and above digits of a password that can comprise of a number, uppercase, and lowercase alphabetical letters.
   ➤ Hit **Next** at the top to continue.

7. Phone Number
   ➤ Carefully choose your Country
   ➤ Type your **Phone Number** for your identity verification.

8. **Verification Method:** Select any of the below options:
   ➤ **Text Message**
   ➤ **Phone Call**
   ➤ Confirm your option with **Checkmark** and hit on **Next**

9. Security Questions
   ➤ Give an unforgettable answer to

the security question you will be asked. You can write the question and the answer into your confidential organizer/planner to subsequently guide you in giving the exact answer whenever you are asked the same question during an essential activity on your iPhone.

10. Verification Code
➢ Type the **Text 6-Digits Code** sent to you through your iPhone Message into the **Verification designated space** for the **Code.**

11. Terms and Conditions
➢ Read through the terms and conditions, digest, and get used to them or familiarize yourself with them because it is very important and hit on **Agree.** If you **Disagree,** that implies that you are not in support of Apple's Terms and Conditions guiding the Apple ID ownership as a result the Apple ID process will be discontinued /terminated.

12. Enter iPhone Passcode: Type your iPhone **Passcode** (4 or 6 digits). If you do not have a passcode, go to the **Add Passcode** page on the section to learn how to create your iPhone Passcode.

13. iCloud
➢ There will be a need for iCloud

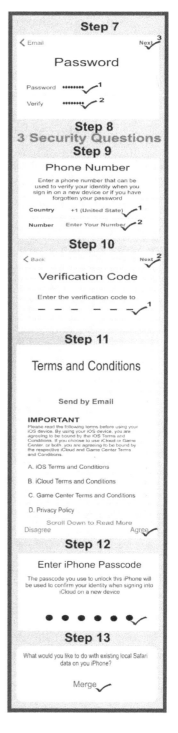

to get documents from Contact, Reminder, Notes, Calendar, and Safari on your iPhone. Therefore, hit on the **Merge** option.

➢ You may consider the other option of **Don't Merge** if you are having any otherwise opinion on their synchronization.

14. Find My iPhone Box

➢ On the box accept by tapping on **OK.**

Hint: You will see your Full Name appear where you saw Sign in to Your iPhone. Anytime you want to sign in to your iPhone hit on your Name and continue.

Now, you have created an Apple ID for yourself. Please you need to keep email & password details carefully to prevent false operators or fraudsters from using your iPhone for illegal activities.

How To Change Your Apple ID Process

Homescreen: Approach the Settings Icon by hitting on it.

Settings: Look at the Profile Name beside Profile Picture at the top hit on **Name.**

Password & Security

➢ Hit on **Change Password**
➢ Type in your valid **Password.**
➢ Type in your **New Password**
➢ Type in your **New Password** again for confirmation
➢ Hit on **Change Password**

How To Sign In Apple ID On Your iPhone Process

Homescreen: Approach the Settings Icon by hitting on it.

Settings: Look at the Profile Name beside Profile Picture at the top hit on **Sign In to Your iPhone.**

Apple ID

- In the Email text field, type your active **Email Address**.
- Look at the top right angle of the screen to hit on **Next.** In the Password text field type in complex and easy to remember **Password.** Better still write it you're your confidential organizer.
- Look at the top right angle of the screen to tap on **Next.**
- In the last part of the page, you will see Sign Out and hit on it to leave the page.

Now, you have added your Apple ID to your iPhone.

How To Recover Your Forgot Apple ID Process

Homescreen: Approach the **Settings Icon** by hitting on it.

Settings: Look at the Profile Name beside Profile Picture at the top hit on **Sign In to Your iPhone.**

Apple ID:

- First and foremost, type your correct Email add into the email text field.
- Look below you will see a 2-in-1 question state thus, Don't have an Apple ID or Forgot it?
- Hit on **Forgot it.**
- **On Informative Box** hit on **Forgot Apple ID.**
- Firstly, you will type in a new

169

Password, and secondly type the same password for the system to verify the correctness.

➢ Go to the top right angle of the screen to tap on **Next.**

You can verify it by tapping on Sign In, Type your submitted email, tap next, type your new approved Password, and tap next.

Perfect Ways of Making Face ID

Face ID is a strong security tool that you can use to prevent fake users from using your iPhone. The use of Face ID on your iPhone will strongly enhance your iPhone security. It can be used to Unlock your iPhone.

You can use Face ID to buy things from iTunes Store, Apple Store, Apple Book with the use of your Apple pay.

Face ID in these modern developed iPhones X has replaced Touch ID in the lower iPhones, as a result, you will see Face ID & Passcode together under Settings on your new iPhone not Touch ID & Passcode.

But, it is less effective among identical twins that are physically looking alike. It will be difficult for your iPhone Face ID infrared sensor to identify or differentiate the facially identical people.

How You Can Create Face ID via Settings Process

Homescreen: Approach the **Settings Icon** by hitting on it.

Settings: Search down to hit on **Set Up Face ID.**

Camera

➢ The Camera should be positioned in a portrait to capture your face. Don't allow any other person to stay behind you when you are taking your face.
➢ Hit on the "**Get Started**" bar.
➢ Let your face be boldly covered in the Camera view center.
➢ Focus your eyes on the Front-Facing Camera Sensor and let your head be in the middle of the round frame on the screen.

➢ As you are turning your head gradually the surrounding lines of the round frame will be changing to green, keep turning your head and let every side of your head be captured by the Camera sensor till the surrounding lines are completely changed to green.

➢ If the first Face ID scanner is successful, hit on the **Continue** bar and turn your head in either the same or opposite way again, once the second Face ID scanner is complete, hit on the **Done** bar.

Hint: If you are unable to turn your head or stiff neck, hit on **Accessibility.**

How to Create a Strong & Safe Passcode

Most of the time your iPhone will always ask you to create a personal Passcode to alternate Face ID to unlock your iPhone. In a situation that you are having an identical twin-face that the Face ID may compromise, you should have a Passcode that is only known to you, then you can use the Passcode to prevent your twin from accessing your iPhone without your consent.

In a situation whereby the Face ID failed to identify your face because of the face transformation you applied (i.e. face mask, excessive face makeup, etc.) then automatically your iPhone will request for your iPhone instead.

Surely, your iPhone will ask for a Passcode anytime you perform the below tasks on your iPhone:

➢ For Installation of iOS
➢ Restarting or Switching On of Your iPhone.
➢ To Remove/Delete All The Data on Your iPhone.
➢ To Change or Access Passcode Settings on Your iPhone.
➢ To Perform Software Update.

How You Can Create Passcode via Settings Process

Homescreen: Approach the **Settings Icon** by hitting on it.

171

Settings: Search down the page and select the **Face ID & Passcode** option.

Face ID & Passcode

➢ Search down the page hit on **Turn Passcode On** option.
➢ By default, you will see 6 digits passcode which you can change to a 4-digits passcode.
➢ But, if you are comfortable with the 6-digits type, then input a complex **Passcode** that will have the mixture of Number, Small Case, and Capital Case of Alphabets.
➢ For 4-digits Passcode, hit on **Passcode Options** above the Keyboard and tap on the third option.
 ✓ A Custom Alphanumeric Code
 ✓ A Custom Numeric Code
 ✓ **4-Digit Numeric Code**
➢ Re-type the complex Passcode for confirmation

Hint: You have to make your Passcode to be complex to prevent passcode hackers or guessers from predicting your passcode. Therefore, mix the passcode digits by selecting **Alphanumeric Code** and write it on your planner for record purposes.

Have you suspected that your present Passcode has been exposed to the wrong person?

Are you noticing suspicious operations on your iPhone?

Then, take a protective wise approach by changing the present passcode to a new Passcode.

How To Change Exposed Present Passcode Process

Homescreen: Hit on **Settings Icon.**

Settings: Search down the page and select the **Face ID & Passcode** option.

Face ID & Passcode: Search down the page and hit on the **Change Passcode** option.

Change Passcode:

- If you are using 6 or 4-Digits Password, type the insecure Password.
- The New Passcode will be requested to be re-typed twice.

Once you type the last digit, it will automatically approve and move to the previous page.

How to Enable Apps in iCloud Account

The activation of apps in the iCloud account will determine the number of apps data that will be automatically uploaded and stored in iCloud storage for you to access them from all your devices. There are lots of suggested apps on your iPhone you can backup and store in the iCloud storage.

This can only be done if you switch on those apps on the iCloud page. Follow the below steps to select the appropriate apps that you want to back up with iCloud.

Therefore, you have to make more storage space available on your iPhone.

The example of the Apps is *Photo, Mail, Contacts, Calendars, Reminders, Notes, Messages, Safari, News, Stocks, Home, Health, Wallet, Game Center, and Siri.*

Homescreen: Approach the **Settings Icon** by hitting on it.

Settings: Look at the Profile Name beside Profile Picture at the top hit on **Sign In to Your iPhone.**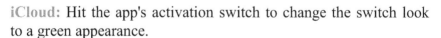

Apple ID: Look at the middle of the page and hit on the **iCloud** option.

iCloud: Hit the app's activation switch to change the switch look to a green appearance.

Keychain:

- Hit on **Keychain** to turn "On" the **iCloud Keychain** switch.

➢ Return to the iCloud page by tapping on the **Back Arrow of iCloud** at the top left angle of the screen.

Hint: In all the devices you are using, it will constantly retain the credit card details and password you have accepted.

Find My iPhone

➢ Select **Find My iPhone** below the Keychain option under iCloud.
➢ Hit on the **Find My iPhone** switch to activate it.
➢ Return to the iCloud page by tapping on the **Back Arrow of iCloud** at the top left angle of the screen.

Hint: This will enable you to locate, lock, activate, or erase your iPhone and other approved equipment if you produce your **Password**.

iCloud Backup

➢ Select **iCloud Backup** option
➢ Hit on **iCloud Backup** to activate the backup.
➢ Return to the iCloud page by tapping on the **Back Arrow of iCloud** at the top left angle of the screen.

iCloud Drive: It will accept all apps to store data and documents in iCloud.

➢ Hit on **iCloud Drive** to activate it.
➢ Move to the top left of the page to tap on the **Back icon** of Apple ID.
➢ Hit on the **Back icon** at the top of Settings and swipe up from the center bottom of the iPhone to go back to the Homescreen.

CHAPTER TEN

How You Can Find Your Lost iPhone

Find My App could not be active without being initially activated through the Settings App. Therefore, for you to make the feature of Find My App to be functional do the following steps.

1. Find Friends and Family Members or
2. Share your location with others
3. Set up **Find My.**

How You Can Activate **Find My** on Your iPhone

Hint: "**Find My**" is automatically turned on when you Sign In your new iPhone with your Apple ID, but, there is a need for you to find out if **Find My iPhone, Enable Offline Finding** and **Send Last Location** are activated.

Homescreen: Hit on **Settings**

Settings: Hit on your **Name/Sign In To Your iPhone** beside the profile picture.

Apple ID: Hit on **Find My**

Find My

> ➢ Hit on **Find My iPhone** to select "**On**" if the activation feature is **Off.**
> **Find My iPhone:** Turn On the

175

activators of the following if they are Off:

- ✓ **Find My iPhone:** It will always request your Password to locate, erase, or lock your iPhone.
- ✓ **Enable Offline Finding:** Your iPhone will be located even when it is not connected to a cellular or Wi-Fi network.
- ✓ **Send Last Location:** iCloud will automatically send the location of your iPhone to Apple when the battery is drastically low.

➤ Hit on **My Location** to select **This Device.**
➤ Hit on **Share My Location's** Activator to put On the switch.

What To Do After You Have Lost Your iPhone

There is a possibility of misplacing your iPhone in a location that you could not recollect because you had visited more than three places before you could remember that your iPhone is missing or it was stolen by a thief.

Also, you might have kept the iPhone in a compartment that is best known to you only but after a while, you could not remember specifically where exactly you had hidden the iPhone.

However, Apple has made a reliable way of locating your iPhone with the use of Find My iPhone and iCloud Map Detection or Google Map to specifically describe and identify the location of your iPhone wherever it had been kept.

First Finding Solution

On Mac or PC

➤ Use any of the available browsers such as Chrome, Mozilla Firefox, Internet Explorer, Safari, Opera, Lynx, or Konqueror.
➤ In the Web Add text field type **icloud.com.**

iCloud Homepage:

➢ Sign In with your Apple ID which includes your **Email** and **Password**.

➢ Click on **Find iPhone Icon**  among the icons on the screen.

iCloud Find My iPhone: Location Map will display on the screen.

➢ At the top **bar** center of the screen click on All Devices.

➢ On the **drop-down & select your iPhone**. (If you are using more than one Apple device that is using the same Apple ID. You will see all the Apple devices on the drop-down).

➢ The Map will zoom out to indicate the iPhone location with a black circle and your iPhone' Name label

➢ At the right corner, you will see 3 options you can use to help your findings
  ✓ Play Sound
  ✓ Lost Mode
  ✓ Erase iPhone

Play Sound: If you pretty sure that the iPhone is around (home, workshop,

177

or office) then you can click **Play Sound** immediately you will start hearing vibration with sound. The sound will continue until you hit on **Find My iPhone Alert** OK.

Lost Mode: This option perfect when you discovered that you can no longer recover/find your iPhone again then you can click on **Lost Mode.**

✓ **Phone Number Dialog Box:** Type your **Phone Number** (that can be called by the finder) and click on **Next** at the top right corner of the dialog box.

✓ Click on the Text box, type the message that will be shown on your iPhone 12 screen. e.g. **"Please I have lost this iPhone. Kindly Call Me. Thank you"** and click on **Done** at the top right angle of the dialog box.

Automatically the iPhone will be locked. It will only be unlocked if you enter your passcode or through your Face ID.

Erase iPhone: This option is accurate when you realized that the iPhone could not be located, then, click **Erase iPhone** to completely remove all your vital and confidential **data, applications (apps) & documents** from the iPhone quickly.

Second Finding Solution:

This is can be used when you are having Google Map App on your iPhone but if do not have the app you can use the iCloud method above.

On Mac or PC

➢ Use any of the available browsers such as Chrome, Mozilla Firefox, Internet Explorer, Safari, Opera, Lynx, or Konqueror.

➢ In the Web Add text field type **www.google.com/maps**

Google Maps:

178

➤ Click on **Menu Icon** at the top left side of the **Search Google Maps Text Field**.

➤ **Menu:** Select **Your Timeline** (Timeline will show various locations you have been with your iPhone on Google maps with an indication of red color).

➤ At the left side of the screen click on **Today** at the front of the **Timeline**.

Immediately a line will displace your different movement today on Google maps to know where your iPhone could be found.

➤ You can zoom in on the map to make the location to be closer and clearer for you to see the location very well.

➤ You can increase the displacement line (appear in blue) at the left side of the screen to see more of different places with their specific time in hours, minutes, and seconds that you moved from a particular place to another place till the final place where the iPhone could be found.

Note: You won't see the exact spot where the iPhone could be found on the Google map but you could only know the environment where you can see the iPhone.

179

How You Can Use Another iPhone to Track

Your Lost iPhone

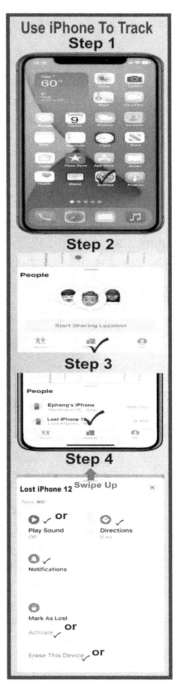

The method of tracking your lost iPhone on the computer is virtually the same as the method and processes of locating your lost iPhone on another iPhone.

If you are having two iPhones in your family or your friend is have one, you can easily use the available iPhone to quickly discover where your iPhone is kept or the location at which it could be found with either hope of recovery or not.

Homescreen: Hit on **Find My** App Icon

Find My: Hit on the **Devices** icon at the bottom center of your iPhone.

Devices: Hit on your lost **iPhone 12's Name** (e.g. Ephong's iPhone) that is your first name will be used to qualified the lost iPhone.

iPhone 12's Name: Swipe up from the top edge center of the page to select one of the available options below:

1. **Play Sound**: Having 100% assurance of finding it.
2. **Directions**: If it is discovered on the map and you want it to be tracked down,
3. **Notifications:** You will be

notified when the iPhone is found.

4. **Mark As Lost**: If the recovery chances of your iPhone is 70 – 80% but the location on the map displayed is extremely far. Then you can hit on **Active.**

5. **Erase This Device**: If the chance of recovering your iPhone is less than 50% which is very narrow, then you can choose the option by tapping it.

Hint: if you eventually selected **Erase This Device** because you have initially lost hope of finding it, as a result, you would not be able to track your iPhone again. But, if by slim opportunity you found the iPhone, you will only be able to restore all the erased data and documents on your iPhone through iCloud backup.

How You Can Share Your Location with Others

You will need to select the people that you wanted to share your location with. This option will enable you to track down your lost iPhone on your friend's iPhone.

Homescreen: Hit on **Find My App Icon**

Find My: Hit on the **People** icon at the bottom left of the screen.

181

Start Sharing Location

> ➤ Type the **Name of the Person** you want to share your location into the Text Field and hit on **Send** at the top right angle of the page.
> ➤ An Optional Dialog Box will show up to select "time for the sharing of your location with the person". Select any of the flowing options:
>> ✓ Share for One Hour
>> ✓ Share Until End of Day
>> ✓ Share Indefinitely
> ➤ Notification: On a Dialog box you will see "You Shared Your Location with the Person's Contact. Hit on **OK.**

How to Use Your iPhone IMEI Code to Block Your Lost iPhone

Your iPhone IMEI Code is very important to you when your iPhone has been confirmed lost and no hope of recovery.

It is very essential to know your iPhone IMEI code that serves as the main personal Apple device identification.

You could use your IMEI code to confirm if your iPhone is originally manufactured by Apple Company or being produced by a fake manufacturer. It can also be used to unlock your iPhone.

Therefore, you have to take the following wise step to confirm your iPhone IMEI code:

Homescreen: Hit on the **Phone App**.

Phone Page:

> ➤ Dial **Asterisk "*", Harsh "#", Zero "0", Six "6", Asterisk "*", Hash "#"** (i.e. *#06#*) on Keypad.

> ➤ Tap on the **Call button**.

➢ Immediately, the IMEI code will appear on your iPhone screen.

Keep the IMEI Code in a confidential planner.

Call your Phone Operator, report the lost iPhone, and dictate your iPhone IMEI code for the lost iPhone to be blocked.

How You Can Setup CarPlay Connection on Your iPhone & Car Stereo

You need to confirm if your car is supporting Apple CarPlay before you start the connection process.

What to Do First
➢ Confirm the CarPlay compatibility with your Stereo.
➢ Verify if the use of CarPlay is allowed in your area or Country.
➢ Start your car, let the screen stereo boot, and show the Homescreen.
➢ Perform your iPhone Settings for CarPlay
➢ Activate Siri.

Activate Siri On Your iPhone

Homescreen: Hit on **Settings**

Settings: Hit on **Siri & Search**

Siri & Search: Put On all the activators.

Different Ways of Connecting CarPlay from Your iPhone 12 to Your Car
1. Lightning to USB cable connection.
2. Bluetooth connection.
3. Wireless connection.

Connection Process for USB Car Port

- Start your Car and let the Car's Stereo boot to the Homepage.
- Insert the small power connector of the USB cable to your iPhone USB power port. Ensure you hear a clear click sound,
- Insert the second end of the USB cord into the Stereo USB port.
- **Once it is properly connected:** You will see the **Apple CarPlay** icon among the Apps icon on the Car's Homescreen.

Connection Process for Car Using Wireless or Bluetooth

- Press and hold down the **Voice-Command** on the Steering Wheel.
- **Go to Your iPhone**

  Homescreen: Hit on Settings.

  Settings: Scroll down to hit on **General**

  General: Hit on **CarPlay**

  CarPlay

- Hit on **Available Car**
- Select your Car name.
- **Once it is connected:** You will see all the **Apple CarPlay** Icon among the Apps icon on the Car's Homescreen.

On Your Touch Sensitive Stereo

➢ The stereo will restart and show **Caution** information, read and hit on **I Agree**

➢ In few seconds the **Apple CarPLay** icon will show.

➢ Hit on the **Apple CarPlay.** All your iPhone Apps (e.g. Call, Music, Messages, Maps, Audiobooks, YouTube, etc.) will display on the Stereo CarPlay Screen. Press the bottom right arrow to see more Apps.

To Add More App to the Default Apps on Your Touch Sensitive Stereo Homescreen

Homescreen: Hit on Settings.

Settings: Scroll down to hit on **General**

General: Hit on **CarPlay**

CarPlay: Select the Name of your Car (e.g. **SUBARU**)

SUBARU: Hit on **Customize**

Customize: Scroll down the page and select from the Apps under **MORE APP** by tapping on the Add Sign in a green circle in front of the App you want to be added on the Car Stereo Homescreen.

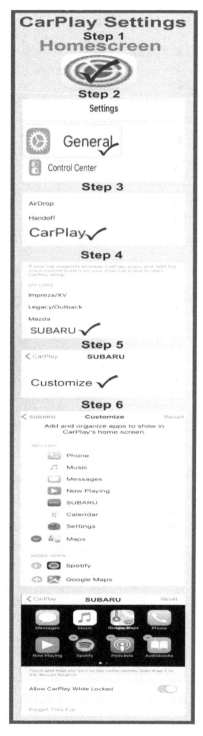 You can also add Google

Map to complement Apple Map.

To Remove Apps: Under the **INCLUDE** list of all the default apps on the Car's Homescreen hit on Minus Sign to in a red circle ⊖ at the front of the App to delete the App from the list. You can restore it by going to MORE APP and hit on the **Add sign**.

How You Can Rearrange The Apps On The CarPlay Homescreen

Customize: Hit on the App and drag it either up or down within the Apps. The Apps will show on the CarPlay Homescreen exactly you arranged them on the **Customized List.**

How You Can Use Siri to Assist You on CarPlay Operation

Siri is very helpful in giving reliable suggestions through the CarPlay to let you know the possible next line of actions or sending a message to someone by dictating your message directly.

You can instruct Siri to forward a call to any of your favorite contacts.

However, the type of your car will determine how you can use Siri to do what you want it to do for you.

There three major ways you can use Siri with your CarPlay.
1. On the Stereo Sensitive Touchscreen touch and hold **CarPlay Home** and ask Siri to do it for you.
2. On the Stereo Sensitive Touchscreen touch and hold **CarPlay Dashboard** and give Siri instruction.
3. On the **Steering Wheel** press and hold the **Voice-Command button** and ask Siri what you wanted.

To Send Message On CarPlay Through Siri

Homescreen: Hit on the **Messages App** icon

Messages: Select the **Name of the Person** you want to send a message to. You can press the up and down arrow to search for the recipient's name up and down of the screen.

Siri icon will appear to send your message. Then dictate your message and Siri will repeat the dictated message back for confirmation.

If what you have said were correct, you can say "Perfect" and order, Siri, to "Send the message". Siri will reply to you that your message has been sent.

How You Can Setup 3D Map Guide

CarPlay Homescreen: Hit on **Map** icon

Map: Hit on **Destinations** at the top right of the screen

Destination: Select from any of these destinations:

1. **Get directions to a destination in the list:** Choose your Destination by tapping.
2. **Get direction to a nearby service:** Choose Service Category including Coffee, Gas or Parking; and choose the destination.

OR

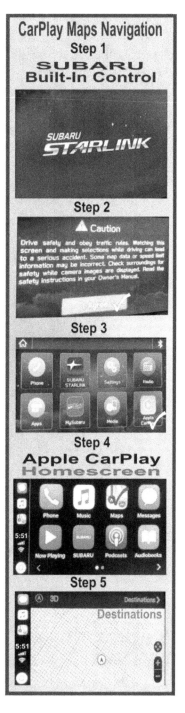

187

Use Siri: Ask Siri:

> ➢ Take me to the address at the destination.
> ➢ Take me home
> ➢ Take me to the nearest fueling station or gas station
> ➢ Take me to the nearest hospital
> ➢ Take me to the nearest Shopping Mall
> ➢ Find the nearest hotel
> ➢ Tell me the location of where I am … and many others.

How You Can Use Map on Your iPhone

Homescreen: Hit on the **Maps** icon.

Maps: Hit on **Directions**

Directions: Select

> ✓ **Drive:** If you are driving
> ✓ **Walk:** If you want to trek the distance
> ✓ **Transit:** If you will be taking various transport
> ✓ **Ride:** If you want to embark on the distance with bicycle, motorcycle, or tricycle.
>
> ➢ Choose the route you want. Maps will show you the shortest direction with consideration of traffic conditions.
> ➢ Hi on **Go.** For you to see the general overview of your route bearing direction.
> ➢ Hit on **Tap for Overview** in the banner. Also, you may hit on **Share ETA** to share your location with others.
> ➢ To stop the **Navigation** hit on **End** and hit on **End Route.**

Use Siri: Ask Siri to "**Stop Navigating**" once you have **Hands-Free Activated** (Switched "ON").

How You Can Prevent Tolls or Highways

Homescreen: Hit on **Settings**

Settings: Hit on **Maps**

Maps: Hit on **Driving & Navigation**

Driving & Navigation: Hit the Activator of **Tolls or Highways**

Hint: As soon as you commence your movement, the Maps will automatically update itself to show you the most appropriate direction.

The hindrance on your route bearing could be seen on Maps iPhone by using your finger to scroll up.

Maps will prevent you from missing your predictive turn at the beginning and walking out of the route by showing you the perfect lane you should remain in when you are driving.

CHAPTER ELEVEN

How Your Health Can be Accurately Tracked with Health App on Your iPhone

To a maximum distinction, your health condition could be guided and monitored through the use of the Health App on your iPhone 12, Mini, Pro, and Max.

It is very easy to apply and operate the feature on the latest iOS 14 to sensor your health history and provide précised past, present, and future data if you accurately entered your detail into the medical profile provided.

For instance, Health App automatically tracks your daily distance running exercise, gradual physical steps, walk, sleep, mental stability, fertility status, diets, weight balance… and several others. If you are also having Apple Watch it could perform the same function of tracking your daily activities and generate relative data to compare with the previous days.

More data could be gotten from all your relevant Apps such as Workout, HealthFit, MySwimPro, Runtastic, Gymaholic, MyNetDiary, iSmoothRun, ManMyRun… and more other Sources that are helping you in organizing your daily activities and execution of health projects or budgets daily, weekly, monthly, or yearly.

In some cases like a heart condition, menstrual cycle… and others, it is very important you use the Apple Watch with your iPhone running with iOS 14 to get perfect prediction and full benefits of the innovativeness and efficiency loaded in the Health App.

Below you will be gradually taken through easy steps of entering your details in the Health App, uses of the donor features, appropriate Apple watch, medical emergency setup link, and tracking of all important activities. All you need to do is to calmly follow those steps below one after the other to achieve all your expected needs.

What To Do First

You will need to provide your Medical Details in these three profile sections:

1. **Health Profile:** It contains your Name, Contact, Date of Birth, Sex, Blood Type, Fitzpatrick Skin Type, and Wheelchair.
2. **Medical ID:** It shows the same Emergency information on your iPhone or Apple watch which also contains activation of Emergency when your iPhone is Locked, Date of Birth (DOB), Medical Conditions, Medical Notes, Allergies & Reactions, Medication, Blood Type, Organ Donor, Weight, Height, and Emergency Contacts.
3. **Organ Donation:** This will enable you to register for an Organ donor through the **sign up with Donate Life.** It comprises the following data of yours; Names, DOB, Last 4 Social Security Number (SSN), Email, Address, ZIP, and Sex.

How Health Profile Can Be Setup On Your iPhone

The setup of the Health App is slightly different from iOS to iOS. If your previous iPhone is running with iOS 12 or 13 the welcome process will be a little different from the starting process of iPhone 12 that is running with the latest iOS 14.

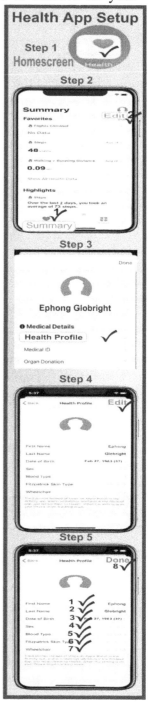

However, all you need to do is very simple; just promptly follow through the welcome steps as they come up on your iPhone Health Page.

But the major setup processes (steps) of registering your essential profile to make the Health App active and do what you wanted will be fully discussed below.

Health App Setup Steps:

Homescreen: Hit on the **Health App** icon.

Health: Hit on **Summary Tab**.

Summary: Hit on your **Profile Picture** at the top right side of the page.

Your Name Page: Hit on **Health Profile**

Health Profile:

- ➢ Hit on **Edit** at the top right angle of the page.
- ➢ Provide your Age, Weight, and Height
- ➢ Hit on **Done** at the top right angle of the page

How Medical ID Can Be Activated On Your iPhone

Homescreen: Hit on the **Health App** icon.

Today Page: Hit on the **Medical ID icon** at the right bottom of the screen ✻

Medical ID: Hit on the **Create Medical ID** bar.

✻ Medical ID

- ➢ Hit on **Show When Locked** activation slider to enable to access Emergency when your iPhone is locked.

- ➢ Hit on **Add Photo** to upload your photo on the page
- ➢ Hit on **Add Date of Birth:** You will see the date suggested at the bottom of the screen. Scroll up until you will get to your Month/Day/Year and hit on it to select.
- ➢ Hit on **Medical Condition** to type your health discomfort (e.g. Herpes, Stomach ache, Arthritis, etc.).
- ➢ Hit on **Medical Notes** to write medical history.
- ➢ Hit on **Allergies & Reactions** to write the signs and symptoms in the text field. I do not have any reaction you may write "Nil/None".
- ➢ Hit on **Medication** to write the doctor's prescription on the text field. If you do not have, you may type "Nil/None"
- ➢ Hit on **Add Blood Type** to select.
- ➢ Hit on **Organ Donor** to select "No, Yes or Not Yet"
- ➢ Hit on **Weight** to select your body weight
- ➢ Hit on **Height** to select your height.
- ➢ Hit on **Add Emergency Contact** to select your trusted loved ones' contact from your iPhone contact list. You can add many favorite contacts.
- ➢ Hit on **Done** at the right top angle of the screen.

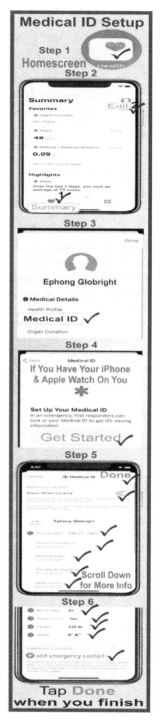

To Confirm How The Emergency Settings Work

➤ Press the **Power** Button to sleep and re-press the button to wake the iPhone.

➤ Use your Face ID to unlock the iPhone.

➤ Swipe up from the bottom center of the screen to see the lock screen with the **Emergency** at the bottom left of the screen.

➤ Hit on the **Emergency**

➤ **Emergency Call:** If you must access Medical ID, then hit the **Medical ID** at the bottom left of the screen. All the information you have provided during the setup.

➤ At the bottom of the Medical ID page, you will see the **Continue bar**. Hit on the **Continue** bar to complete the registration.

➤ Hit on **Complete Registration with Donate later** bar.

➤ **Thank You:** Hit on the **Done** bar.

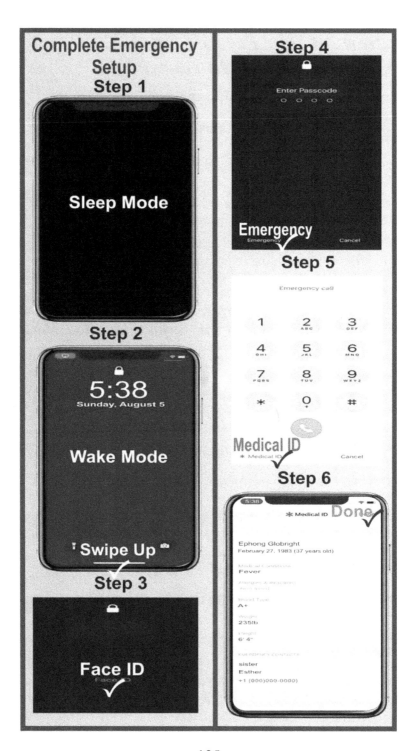

Complete Emergency Setup

Step 1

Sleep Mode

Step 2

5:38
Sunday, August 5

Wake Mode

Swipe Up

Step 3

Face ID

Step 4

Enter Passcode

Emergency   Cancel

Step 5

Emergency call

1	2 ABC	3 DEF
4 GHI	5 JKL	6 MNO
7 PQRS	8 TUV	9 WXYZ
*	0	#

Medical ID
* Medical ID   Cancel

Step 6

5:38   * Medical ID   Done

Ephong Globright
February 27, 1983 (37 years old)

Medical Conditions
Fever

Allergies & Reactions
Penicillin

Blood Type
A+

Weight
235lb

Height
6' 4"

EMERGENCY CONTACTS
sister
Esther
+1 (000)000-0000

195

How All Your Favorite Categories Can Be Tracked On Your iPhone

Homescreen: Hit on the **Health App** icon

Today Summary: Hit on **Summary Tab**

Summary: Hit on **Edit** at the top right angle of the screen page.

Edit Favorite

- ➢ Hit on each desirable Star to add more **Categories.** ⭐ .
- ➢ As soon as you have completely selected all your preferred **Favorite Categories**, hit on the **Done** at the top right side of the screen.

Hint: When you hit on each star, it will change from frame star ☆ to full blue star ⭐ .

How Organ Donation Can Be Enabled On Your iPhone

Homescreen: Hit on the **Health App** icon.

Health: Hit on **Summary Tab**.

Summary: Hit on your **Profile Picture** at the top right side of the page.

Your Name Page: Select **Organ Donor**

Organ Donor: Hit on the **Sign Up with Donate Life** bar to sign up.

Registration

- ➢ All your profile details will display, what you only need is to enter the last four-digit number of your **Social Security Number** (SSN).

- ➢ Hit on the **Continue** button below to complete your registration.
- ➢ Hit on **Complete Registration with Donate Life** at the bottom center of the screen.
- ➢ **Thank You:** Hit on the **Done** button below.
- ➢ Your complete registration with Donate Life will show up under your Medical ID profile as **Organ Donor-Donate Life.**

How to Fix Failure of Health Tracking Feature on Your iPhone

For your health tracking steps to be functionally perfect, you need to connect your Apple Watch with your iPhone.

If you are having a challenge of not seeing your steps being tracked by the Health App on your iPhone, then take the following steps:

Homescreen: Hit on the **Health App** icon.

Health: Hit on **Summary Tab**.

Summary: Hit on your **Profile Picture** at the top right side of the page.

Your Name Page: Under **Privacy** hit on **Devices**

Devices: Select your **Apple Watch**

Your Watch Privacy: Hit on **Privacy Settings** and activate **Fitness Tracking** by switching On the Activator.

How Family Sharing Can Be Setup on Your iPhone

Homescreen: Hit on the **Settings App** icon

Settings: Go to your **Profile Name** at the top

Apple ID: Select Set Up Family Sharing

Family Sharing: Hit on the "**Get Started**" button

Get Started: Select **Location Sharing** or any other feature you want to share. There might be a slightly different method of setup in various other features of family sharing available.

Share Your Location with Your Family: Hit on the **Share Your Location** button at the bottom center of the screen. If you are not ready to share your location you can select the **Not Now** option below.

Invite Your Family: Hit on the **Invite Family Members** bar at the bottom center.

Family Sharing Setup

Step 1

Homescreen

Step 2

Settings

Ephong Globright
Apple ID, iCloud, iTunes & App Store

Airplane Mode
Wi-Fi
Bluetooth
Cellular
Personal Hotspot

Notifications
Control Center
Do Not Disturb

General

Step 2

Apple ID

Ephong Globright

Name, Phone Numbers, Email
Password & Security
Payment & Shipping

iCloud
Set Up Family Sharing...

iPhone
iPad

Step 3

Family Sharing

Share music, movies, apps, storage and more with up to six members of your family.

You'll also get a family photo album, family calendar, and access to family devices in Find My iPhone.

Get Started

Step 4

Get Started

Choose the first feature you'd like to share with your family.

iTunes & App Store Purchases

Apple Music

iCloud Storage

Location Sharing

Step 5

Share Your Location with Your Family

Set up location sharing so that everyone in your family can view each others' location in Find My Friends and Messages.

Family members will also see the location of each others' devices in Find My iPhone.

Share Your Location

Step 6

Invite Your Family

Use Messages to invite up to five other people to join your family and share their location with you.

Invite Family Members

200

How Your Menstrual Cycle Can Be Tracked On Your iPhone

The use of Health apps to track women's menstrual cycle can be fully studied and determined on your iPhone since the iPhone came with iOS 14 can effectively use Apple watch running with watchOS 6 to effectively complement your health reading and tracking.

Apple Watch is perfectly used to get an accurate reading of your heartbeat, rate, and general health conditions.

How You Can Set Up Every Month Menstrual Cycle on Your iPhone

Homescreen: Hit on the **Health App** icon.

Search: Hit on the **Browse** tab at the bottom right of the screen.

Browse:

> ➢ Select **Cycle Tracking** among the **Health Categories**
> ➢ Hit on the "**Get Started**" button.

Cycle Tracking: Hit on **Options**

Options

> ➢ You will scroll down to select **Period Length** and swipe up to select your period duration e.g. 2 days, 3 days, 4 days, 5days, etc. The period length is the number of days you experience menstrual flow. For example, If you see the menstrual flow from Aug 2 to 5 is equal to 4days.
> ➢ Select **Cycle Length** and swipe up to select the appropriate days before the next menstrual cycle e.g. 25 days or 26 days etc.

Hint: If you are having some pre or post symptoms that come with your cycle you may activate all the relevant suggested contents above **Your Cycle Log.** Some of them are:

1. Spotting
2. Basal Body Temperature
3. Cervical Mucus Quality
4. Ovulation Test Result
5. Sexual Activity
6. Symptoms… and others.

How You Can See Your Cycle Timeline

Homescreen: Hit on the **Health App** icon.

Search: Hit on the **Browse** tab at the bottom right of the screen.

Browse: Select **Cycle Tracking** among the **Health Categories**

The Timeline will appear as:

1. **Solid Circles**: Number of days you recorded for your menstrual period.
2. **Purple Dots**: The number of days you recorded for experiencing symptoms
3. **Light Red Circle:** This is your next menstrual period Prediction.
   - ✓ **For You to Hide or Display Predicted Period Days:** Select **Option** and activate the **Period Prediction** switch.
4. **Light Blue Days:** These predict your possible Fertility Window. You should not use it to guide yourself for birth control.
   - ✓ **For You to Hide or Display Infertility Window:** Select **Option** and activate the **Fertility Prediction** switch.

How You Can Know Your Possible Next Menstrual Cycle

Homescreen: Hit on the **Health App** icon.

Search: Hit on the **Browse** tab at the bottom right of the screen.

Browse: Select **Cycle Tracking** among the **Health Categories**

Cycle Tracking

> ➢ Scroll down to select **Prediction** under **Cycle Log.** This will enable you to know your next menstrual cycle.
>> ✓ **If you are unable to see the evaluation:** Select **Show All** before the prediction option.
> ➢ Scroll down to select **Statistics.** This will enable you to see all your previous menstrual period and predictive cycle length.

On Apple Watch: For You To Determine Date

> ➢ Launch the **Cycle Track App.**
> ➢ Scroll down to select **Period Prediction/Last Menstrual Period.**

How You Can Track All Your Cycle Symptoms in Health App

Homescreen: Hit on the **Health App** icon.

Search: Hit on the **Browse** tab at the bottom right of the screen.

Browse: Select **Cycle Tracking** among the **Health Categories**

Cycle Tracking**:** Hit on **Options** at front of **Cycle Log**

Options: Activate the **Symptoms** activator ⬭ to access all the possible symptoms before/during/after the menstrual cycle. All the symptoms are listed below:

- ✓ Abdominal Cramp
- ✓ Acne
- ✓ Appetite
- ✓ Bloating
- ✓ Breast Tenderness
- ✓ Constipation
- ✓ Diarrhea
- ✓ Headache
- ✓ Hot Flashes
- ✓ Lower Back Pain
- ✓ Mood Changes
- ✓ Nausea
- ✓ Ovulation Pain
- ✓ Tiredness
- ✓ Sleep Changes

You can tap on any of the symptoms you are experiencing before or during or after the menstrual cycle to log your symptoms with Cycle Tracking.

How You Can Record Menstrual Cycle Symptoms on Your Apple Watch.

On Apple Watch:

- ➤ To launch Apple tray by pressing **Digital Crown**

- ➤ Select the **Cycle Tracking** App icon
- ➤ Hit on **Symptoms**
- ➤ Scroll through the various available symptoms and hit on various symptoms lists you regularly experience before or during or after the menstrual cycle.
- ➤ Hit on **Done**

How You Can Set Up Prediction for Period, fertility, and Notification, through Cycle Tracking

How You Can Track All Your Cycle Symptoms in Health App

Homescreen: Hit on the **Health App** icon.

Search: Hit on the **Browse** tab at the bottom right of the screen.

Browse: Select **Cycle Tracking** among the **Health Categories**

Cycle Tracking: Hit on **Options**

Options: Hit on the activator of the below features to turn them "On".

- ➤ Activate **Period Prediction**.
- ➤ Activate the **Period Notification.**
- ➤ Activate the **Fertility Predictions**
- ➤ Activate **Fertility Notifications.**

How You Can Record A Period Flow Level Through Cycle Tracking on Your Apple Watch

On Apple Watch

- ➤ To launch Apple tray, press **Digital Crown**

- ➤ Select the **Cycle Tracking** App icon
- ➤ In the everyday tracker above the Data Summary hit on the **Day.**
- ➤ Below Menstrual Unit hit on **Period** to record your menstrual flow. Select your period flow level by tapping on any of these options below:
  - ✓ Light
  - ✓ Medium

205

✓ Heavy

❯ Hit on **Done.**

How You Can Further Record Your Sexual Activity In Cycle Tracking

You can use this to track when last or the period you had sex with your spouse.

Option:

❯ Hit on **Sexual Activity**

❯ On the same page hit on **Sexual Activity** and select **Had Sex**.

❯ Select **Not Used** or **Used** to remind you of your sexual protection.

How You Can Record Your Sexual Activity in Cycle Tracking on Your Apple Watch

On Apple Watch

❯ To launch Apple tray, press **Digital Crown**

❯ Select the **Cycle Tracking** App icon

❯ Hit on **Sexual Activity**

❯ If you had sexual intercourse, then hit on **Had Sex**

❯ For protection confirmation, select **Not Used** or **Used**

How You Can Remove All Cycle Tracking in Health App On Your iPhone.

Homescreen: Hit on the **Health App** icon.

Search: Hit on the **Browse** tab at the bottom right of the screen.

Browse: Select **Cycle Tracking** among the **Health Categories**

Cycle Tracking: Scroll down to select **View Cycle Tracking Items**

View Cycle Tracking Items: Hit on every **Category Log** you wanted to remove.

➢ Scroll down to the bottom region to hit on **Show All Data.**
➢ At the top right angle of the screen hit on **Edit.**
➢ Hit on the **Remove icon** beside the data you wanted to remove.
➢ Hit on **Delete.**
➢ Hit on **Done** at the top right angle of the screen.

How to Get the Source of Your Data from Different Sources

Health App always makes use of the same data from different sources like Apple Watch, iPhone, and iPod. If you are using several Apple devices that are connected with the iPhone, it is very important as a user to specifically know which of the Apple device is responsible for the data making.

You can set your iPhone to be the major source that Health App should be used for data generation, instead of using all available Bluetooth devices. This method is called the **Prioritization of Device.**

Homescreen: Hit on the **Health App** to launch the page.

Summary: Hit on the **Browse** icon tab.

Browse: Hit on a **Category** such as **Activity**.

Activity: Select the **Subcategory** such as Steps or Walk & Running or any other one.

Hint: But if you are unable to see the subcategory you are looking for, then you can scroll up to access the Searching tool at the top of the page. Hit the field and enter the **Subcategory** and it will appear.

Steps: Swipe up to select **Data Sources & Access**

Hint: You will see all the Sources that are responsible for the make of the Steps' Data will be enlisted.

How You Can Access All The General Sources For The Health App

Homescreen: Hit on the **Health App** to launch the page.

Summary: Hit on **Profile Picture** at the top right of the page.

Your Profile Name Page: Move down the page to Privacy and hit on **Apps or Devices.**

You will see all the Sources that enable Health App to generate those Data.

How You Can Assign Sources for Data

This will enable you to prioritize sources for the making of a particular subcategory data in the Health App.

Homescreen: Hit on the **Health App** to launch the page.

Summary: Hit on the **Browse** icon tab.

Browse: Hit on a **Category** such as **Activity**

Activity: Select the **Subcategory**

Subcategory: You will go down the page and select **Data Source & Access.**

Data Source & Access: Hit on **Edit**

- ➤ Touch and Hold down **Change Order** Button at the front of the Data Source.
- ➤ You can either **Drag Up** or **Down** the **Data Source** on the lists.

If you do not want a Data Source to generate Data for the Subcategory: Deactivate the **Activation Switch.**

BONUS CHAPTER

The Protective Accessory for iPhone 12, Mini, Pro & Max

Although, Apple organization has already designed prolong durable iPhone outer ringside to satisfy the user by using a stainless glass body to repel water and easy to clean when it is having contact with hard stain or covered with dust.

But, the is not adequate for those that want the iPhone to be a fully protected incidence that may damage the sensitive screen and the backside of the iPhone.

Apple company only provided partial protection, not total protection that could prevent the iPhone's screen from damage when it suddenly falls on a hard pointed surface. As a result, it very important to provide a more sustainable additional **Screen Protector and quality body Casing**.

Now the choice of providing absolute protection for your iPhone is in your hand. If you are looking for where you could get quality and durable casing or screen protectors, there are many quality and smart iPhone body Case and Screen Protectors on the "Amazon Platform", that will also add beauty to your iPhone look "appearance". Search for anyone you like and make an order.

How to Fix Screen Protector without Bubble on the Screen

Some of the Screen protectors come with a sachet of Wet Wipe and Dry Wipe.

Materials You Need:

Alcohol Swap, or Isopropyl Alcohol, Microfiber Cleaning Cloth (MCC) (e.g., Magicfiber, e-cloth,), Dust Removing Sticker (DRS), Thick Paper Business Card

First Method

1. Switch off your iPhone
2. Use alcohol swap or add small Isopropyl alcohol into clean cotton to clean up the surface of the iPhone screen to remove oil on the screen surface. Ensure you clean from inside to the edges of the iPhone.
3. Use the available MCC to clean the iPhone screen surface from edge to edge to completely remove dust.
4. Use a side of DRS to sweep the screen surface from the top to the bottom of the screen. Just 2 to 3 times (Optional).
5. Remove the protective paper/nylon at the front of the Screen Protector.
6. Gently hold the Screen front the left and right sides with your hand.
7. Slowly bend down the head of the Screen protector toward the head of the iPhone. Use your second hand to support the screen protector at the opposite end to align the screen protector edge with the iPhone top edge.
8. Slowly move your hand holding the screen down; with the help of the thumb of the second-hand press the screen surface to remove any possible bubble and use the Thick Card to slightly press the screen down and sweep the surface toward the bottom of the iPhone side by side as you are moving down your hand to prevent bubble(s).

Second Method

1. Remove the protective nylon or paper on the screen protector surface.
2. Position the side of the screen protector at one side of the iPhone to ensure that the screen is at the center of the iPhone. Some screen protectors come with tape stickers but if you do not have never mind.
3. Position the upper end of the screen protector at the same upper end of your iPhone and gently move down your hand until it gets to the opposite end.
4. Allow it to spread and use the Microfiber Cleaning Cloth to press the screen surface from the top of the iPhone by

moving your hand from left to right till you will get to the bottom of the iPhone to prevent a bubble. **Or**

Third Method: Nylon or Paper Sticker Support Method

➢ If you have a paper sticker, cut three of 4cm of paper sticker each. Stick 2cm from the length of the paper sticker at the left, right, and bottom center.

➢ Gently position the screen protector top edge at the exact top edge of the iPhone screen.

➢ Look at both sides, and ensure the screen protector is aligned with the iPhone edge.

➢ Use the remaining 2cm paper sticker at the left and right to adhere to the screen protector with the main iPhone body.

➢ Hold the opposite paper sticker to slowly bring down the screen protector to the surface of the iPhone.

➢ Use clean soft MCC to rub the surface of the protective screen from left to right to prevent bubbles as shown in the below pictures.

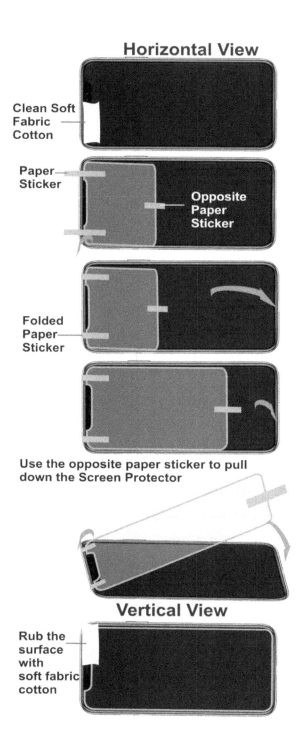

Horizontal View

Clean Soft
Fabric
Cotton

Paper
Sticker

**Opposite
Paper
Sticker**

Folded
Paper
Sticker

**Use the opposite paper sticker to pull
down the Screen Protector**

Vertical View

Rub the
surface
with
soft fabric
cotton

213

www.ingramcontent.com/pod-product-compliance
Lightning Source LLC
La Vergne TN
LVHW051327050326
832903LV00031B/3410